Don't Tell Me the Ending!

An Introductory Text for Aspiring Film Critics

by John Morano

Windstorm Creative
Port Orchard 🎥 Washington

Don't Tell Me the Ending: An Introductory Text for Aspiring Film Critics
copyright 2007 by John Morano
published by Windstorm Creative

ISBN 978-1-59092-659-8
9 8 7 6 5 4 3 2
First edition September 2007

Cover image by Dic Liew.
Design by Buster Blue of Blue Artisans Design.

Printed in the United States of America.

For information about reprint or other subsidiary rights, contact legal@windstormcreative.com

Windstorm Creative is a multiple-imprint, international organization involved in publishing books in all genres, including electronic publications; producing games, toys, videos and audio cassettes as well as producing theatre, film and visual arts events. The wind with the flame center is a trademark of Windstorm Creative.

Windstorm Creative
7419 Ebbert Dr SE
Port Orchard WA 98367
www.windstormcreative.com
360-769-7174 ph

Windstorm Creative is a member of the Orchard Creative Group, Ltd.

Library of Congress Cataloging in Publication data available.

For Martin Severino

Thank you for taking me to the movies, for bringing me to theater,
for giving me reading lists, for sending me books,
for sharing your thoughts and for helping me develop my own.

And thank you for being the type of teacher
who keeps on teaching
long after the bell has rung...

Don't Tell Me the Ending! is first and foremost
for you.

Thank You

I'd like to thank the Monmouth University community for continued, generous support and encouragement to allow this project to be completed. Also, to the many students of *Writing the Review*, who took the course over the years and helped me learn as much about film reviewing as any text I read or class that I attended.

Also, thanks to Matt Mastroilli at *Night & Day Magazine* for permission to use past reviews as material in the text, for his friendship and unwavering support.

Thanks to Clark University's *Scarlet*, the student newspaper, for giving a confused basketball player the chance to write about film.

Thanks to Bob Shartoff, the Creative Director, and Mark Bego, the Editor-in-Chief at *Modern Screen Magazine,* for taking a chance on a young critic 'back in the day.'

Thanks to Gary Phoebus for always being there, often at a moment's notice, when it's time to print a manuscript that can be sent to publishers and readers.

Thanks to Dr. Chad Dell, Dr. Eleanor Novek and my wife, Kris, for listening to my thoughts (even when you have other things to accomplish) and for keeping my work on your radar when you see interesting tidbits.

A special thanks to Jennifer and Cris DiMarco, my publishers, for their lasting, unwavering support of my work. And, for allowing an environmental novelist to jump genres to produce something a little different. It's always a joy working with you.

Thanks to Buster Blue and Dic Liew for design that absolutely enhances the words I've written.

Thanks to Jim Reme, photographer and friend, for always making yourself available to take a 'quick' shot.

As always, thanks to Kris, John and Vincent for putting up with Dad's strange work and strange work habits.

Lastly, thank you Lord for giving me the words...

Table of Contents

Don't Tell Me the Ending!

An Introductory Text for Aspiring Film Critics

by John Morano

Introduction

Don't Tell Me the Ending! is an introductory level textbook intended to provide students and movie goers with useful information to help them express their views of what they've experienced on screen in a style that readers might find in family newspapers and consumer magazines.

This how-to text for aspiring film critics examines the process of viewing films with the intent of producing written reviews. Readers will see how reviews can be structured and what elements these columns might contain or comment on. There is information about planning a career as a film critic, how to gather your material, how to structure a review and other practical advice.

An old adage among moviegoers says, "Check your brains at the door." For some consumers that might actually be the goal of going to the movies, but for critics, there couldn't be a worse piece of advice. As a critic, when you enter the theater, you want to be on your game, and that means all the synapses are firing. Check your coat, check your hat; maybe even your umbrella... but hang onto your brain. You'll be needing it.

While the vast majority of us have seen countless films over the years, the critic takes things a step further, communicating to a mass audience just what the film achieved, where it failed and what the overall effect of the time spent in the theater turned out to be. As simple as this might seem, it's no easy task. There are obligations placed upon the critic from many different constituencies. The critic is expected to serve the readers of the publication and the editors she works for. The critic must also be fair to the filmmakers. And certainly, most critics would admit to an obligation to reasonably advance their careers. There can be situations where these concerns compete, making it difficult to do the job, but they are not commonly exclusive of each other. More often competing constituencies demand careful balance. As one begins to prioritize these obligations, the critic's personal style begins to emerge.

Editors & Publishers

Filmmakers CRITIC'S OBLIGATIONS Self

Readership

Regardless of what filmmakers or other vested individuals might claim, you are not in the business of promotion. A critic must criticize. Of course, you will hopefully balance your criticism with praise in whatever doses the films you cover deserve. French critic/director Francois Truffaut asks a question, "... to those who rail against unfavorable reviews: Would you prefer to take your chances that the critics will never mention you, that your work will not be the subject of a single printed line? Yes or no?" (1) Truffaut brings to mind the adage, "There is no such thing as bad publicity." He points out that those who are prepared to receive praise must also accept criticism. It comes with the territory. The mandate for the critic is to accomplish this task with credibility, honesty and fairness. Dennis Ray Wheaton, chief dining critic for *Chicago* magazine, points out, "...the role of critics is as very important gatekeepers between the public and the people who are producing these cultural works." (2)

With respect to style, there are generally two orders of film critics. One is the reviewer. The reviewer tends to tell readers about the movie, stressing plot synopsis and interesting entertainment tidbits, often centered around the celebrities. These reviews are commonly light on actual criticism. In *The New York Times Film Reviews 1917-1970*, editor George Amberg wrote, "... the reviewer is primarily a journalist concerned with the news of the moment."

The critic tends to be longer on critical analysis and shorter on plot synopsis and pop culture banter. Amberg explains the role of the critic by saying, "... the critic... is primarily an analyst concerned with lasting aesthetic qualities."(3) The dividing line between the two, however, to use Amberg's term, is "fluid".

In *Singularities* the distinguished critic John Simon describes the difference between a reviewer and a critic by writing:

"... a reviewer is someone who has no expertise, standards

or vision beyond those of his readers – or, in the rare case

he has them, keeps them well hidden; a critic is someone who

knows, demands and envisions more than most of his readers.

A critic, in short, is an artist, a teacher, a philosopher. He

writes as well, or nearly, as a novelist, playwright or scriptwriter.

... He is enough of a thinker to perceive connections between

this play, film, opera, ballet, painting or whatnot and the world

and life in general. For all of these reasons he wants his subject

to be a work of art, which is to say entertaining but also significant,

penetrating and somehow revitalizing – and not *only* a piece of

entertainment, which is to say a weapon for killing time.

"...you read a critic as a whetstone: something to sharpen

your own understanding on, either by agreement or disagreement,

in a dialogue."(4)

The style that I have geared this book toward, and that I believe most newspapers and magazines are interested in these days, is a combination of both, perhaps 2/5 reviewer and 3/5 critic; a *criviewer,* if you will. Of course, you're somewhat free to decide whatever mix works best for you and your readers. When you're working professionally, understand that your editors might also exert influence to 'perfect' your style. The editors at *Sesame Street Parents Magazine* are probably looking for a different style of writing, and perhaps a different focus, than the editors at *Rolling Stone*. Having the ability to be flexible with your writing (not necessarily your opinion) will likely get you more opportunity, especially early on.

In *Introduction to Film Criticism*, authors Tim Bywater and Thomas Sobchack write:

> There are a good number of "reviewers" for weekly newspapers and magazines who go beyond the basic function that the simple film review serves. Their articles are often perceptive, offering as much to the reader who has already seen the film under discussion as to the reader who hasn't yet seen it.
>
> Indeed, some of the best writing ever published on film has been written by people who would characterize themselves as journalists rather than as critics or scholars, people who have brought a native, experienced, and humane intelligence to the job of reviewing movies and who have, over the years, become known and respected for their critical abilities.
>
> ...But in the last analysis, the best of the journalistic critics are not copies – they're originals, each with his or her own style and own eccentricity, but all with the ability to bring freshness, immediacy, and vitality to their analysis of movies. (5)

The author assumes that readers have an interest in film; both current and past, both American and foreign, both studio and independent. The author also assumes that readers are interested in expressing their views in print. If both these assumptions are true, and you're just starting your journey down the road of criticism, then *Don't Tell Me the Ending!* should provide the aspiring critic with an informative jumping off point.

An anecdote can occasionally be helpful in a review (or a textbook). When I began covering film I told a friend about my career choice. At first the friend thought it was a fascinating way to make a living, but after we discussed it he wound up saying, "Ah, you're gonna ruin it for yourself."

I asked, "Ruin what?"

"Movies... you'll never be able to enjoy them again. Every time you see a film, you'll be all hyper-critical. No more fun at the movies for you," my friend warned.

I thought about that for a moment and finally disagreed, asking, "Does a chef not enjoy food? Does a great basketball coach not enjoy a good game? Does a political journalist not enjoy a debate?"

My friend stared back at me.

"I might enjoy the film differently as a critic," I continued, "but don't think for a moment that my sensitivity to what's happening on screen lessens my experience. In my mind, it actually enhances it."

"We'll see," my friend said smugly.

I didn't mind his pessimistic premonition. I realized my response was actually directed more to me than him. And after more years than I care to count covering films, I have to admit, I generally still love going to the movies. And it's pretty easy to know when I'm there with a pad on my knee as opposed to popcorn (although both actually work). Lesson number one; if you want to be a critic, it helps to like movies.

"To have my life unpunctuated by the physical act of film-going," writes *The New*

Republic's legendary critic, Stanley Kauffmann in *Why I'm Not Bored* (1974), "is almost like walking with a limp, out of my natural rhythm."(6)

Francois Truffaut recalls his love of movies, saying:

I saw my first two hundred films on the sly, playing hooky
and slipping into the movie houses without paying – through the
emergency exit or the washroom window – or by taking advantage
of my parents' going out for an evening (I had to be in bed,
pretending to be asleep, when they came home). I paid for these
great pleasures with stomachaches, cramps, nervous headaches and
guilty feelings, which only heightened the emotions evoked by the
films. (7)

While I'm certainly not suggesting that young critics engage in 'theft of services,' 'illegal entry' or some form of home espionage, both Truffaut and Kauffmann give one a sense of the passion film can (and perhaps should) ignite in a fledgling critic. Truth be told, I also took advantage of nights when my friends were ushering and/or working the box office at the Criterion Theater on Atlantic Avenue in East Rockaway where I grew up.

After years of writing film reviews, maybe even months, you'll find that being a critic, talking about other people's work, will actually reveal quite a bit about *you* to readers. That's generally a good thing. It suggests honesty and openness. But it can also be unsettling. In her Introduction to *For Keeps* (1994) Pauline Kael, the controversial *New Yorker* critic, wrote, "I am frequently asked why I don't write my memoirs. I think I have."(8) The critic is saying that if you read her reviews, over time you can't help but learn all about who she is, what she values and other details that make her a unique person.

In the Introduction to *Roger Ebert's Book of Film* (1997), the author comments on the personal exposure of the critic by writing, "... I wouldn't want to give up reading and writing about movies, because the best of such writing is not about the movies anyway: It's about the author."(9) While Ebert's assertion is not completely true, there is a lot of truth to it, and the spirit of the statement is certainly well taken.

The house lights are flashing, the exit doors are closing and the curtain is rising. Find your seat, take out your pen and let's see the show.

Chapter 1

What makes a good film good, or a bad film bad?

"...the critic with taste is not likely to become
enthusiastic about many things he reviews: a
reviewer you see quoted in the advertisements
of every other show is not, you may be assured,
a critic with taste."(1)

John Simon, *Singularities*

Everyone has their own view, their own vision of just what good film is all about. For some people a satisfying trip to the movies means a good cry, for others it's a good laugh. Still others prefer to be taken to 'strange new worlds'. Who's right, who's wrong? How does a critic deal with so many different tastes?

Shakespeare provides some sound advice:

This above all: to thine own self be true,
And it must follow, as the night the day,
Thou canst not then be false to any man.

Hamlet, act I, scene iii, lines 78-80 (2)

But it's not quite that simple for the critic. Critic Craig Seligman writes, "For a critic to address only what she loves is as skewed as it is for her to confront only what she hates." (3) So producing a good review is also a matter of balance. While it's paramount that a critic represent her own thoughts honestly, one must also take into account that certain movies will play to specific audiences, many times an audience that you might not be a part of. The better critics are able to anticipate how a film might play to someone else.

Woody Allen films tend to do much better box-office in large metropolitan centers, especially in the Northeast. Does that mean they're better, or worse, than films with a more general appeal?

First, be careful not to fall into the 'better or worse' trap. You need not label everything better or worse, success or failure, right or wrong. Some things just are... The sky is blue, grass is green and water is wet. No necessity for a value judgement there.

Beware of absolutes and extremes. Phrases like 'never before' or 'the most' or 'totally useless' (this last being redundant) are absolutes. They offer you no escape. A single exception proves you wrong. Whenever appropriate, try to give yourself some breathing room. Overstatement is difficult to defend. Hyperbole will ultimately diminish your credibility and lessen the effect of absolute statements when they are warranted.

John Simon discusses overpraise in *Singularities*, commenting:

The most serious damage of overpraise is not that it may keep a piece of nonsense running longer than it deserves. The real danger is that Crying Wonder can become just as self-defeating as Crying Wolf. There is hardly a reviewer left who hasn't used up and devaluated his entire stock of superlatives. There have been so many miracles, masterworks and unique experiences that the public, duped a thousand times over, has lost faith in all those workaday wonders. Then what happens when a truly wonderful play or film or composition comes along? It has been discovered that though a single powerful reviewer or a large body of ordinary reviewers in negative agreement can scuttle a show, they are less and less able to sell and save one.(4)

On the subject of judgements, beware of a generational bias (among others). Many naive students say things like, "Films today are much more sophisticated than they used to be." Really? I suppose *A Night at the Roxybury* (1998), *Connie and Karla* (2004), *In the Mix* (2005), *Deuce Bigalow: European Gigolo* (2005) and *Phat Girlz* (2006) are classic productions that will outdraw and outlive those lame old black and white films, *Citizen Kane* (1941), *Casablanca* (1942), or *The Philadelphia Story* (1940). Be careful, just because something is new, doesn't mean it's superior. Good critics have a solid sense of film history and try to keep creations in perspective.

Getting back to Woody Allen films, as a critic you should feel free to say whatever you believe about why his films might play in one demographic and not in another, provided you do one thing... support your claim. One of the most common questions I ask my students is, "Why do you say that?" Always remember that by the time a *reader* asks that question it's too late to do anything about it, the confusing comment has already been printed. You can never say to a reader, "You know what I mean." If they're asking why you wrote something, then obviously, they don't know what you meant. So, one of the most important jobs of the critic is to anticipate readers' questions. One way to drastically reduce confusion is to provide support, usually through examples or further explanation, as often as possible. Generally speaking, don't assume that readers will get your point, understand your insinuation or agree with your claim. You're usually better off assuming they won't agree or understand.

Although we didn't always see the same films, my mother and I would sometimes discuss movies. She, a retired first grade teacher, tends to like movies about nice people with happy endings. She rarely misses a Hallmark Hall of Fame television special. Occasionally I'd ask her about a movie and she'd say something like, "I didn't like *Cape Fear*." (Disclosure: I don't think she's ever seen this film .)

I would respond, "Why not?"

She'd answer, "I don't know. I don't like that Robert DeNiro."

"But you loved him in *Awakenings*?"

"He was just so nasty in *Cape Fear*. I don't like that Robert DeNiro anymore."

I'm sure most of you can see where this is going. My mother's line of reasoning is absolutely acceptable for the film consumer. As they say, the customer is always right. But this won't fly for a critic. Because Robert DeNiro was 'so nasty' so successfully, my guess is that my mom, if she actually saw *Cape Fear*, not only saw a good film, but an outstanding performance. If it, in fact, upset her so much that she was willing to write off both the film and the actor... BRAVO! So, keep in mind, just because something frustrates, confuses, disappoints, upsets or disturbs you, does not mean the film is problematic. When a film or any of its elements evokes strong feelings, even unpleasant ones, that can often signal a success.

Saying, "Robert DeNiro had a filthy mouth," or "Robert DeNiro was so violent," raises another problem. Really, DeNiro was neither of those things. His *character* was foul-mouthed and violent. Try not to confuse actor with character. They're really two separate people.

Another question many critics ask themselves before writing up a film is, "What league is this picture in?" One way to answer that is to look at the movie's budget, although many low-budget films can become huge successes and vice-versa. Is the film professionally done? Is it a student film? Is it an independent production, a foreign film? There are some differences between the resources behind *Titanic* (1997) and *The Blair Witch Project* (1999). Certainly, in the end, the film will stand or fall on its own merits, but recognizing budgetary and professional differences might help one produce a more enlightened review, providing context to the question, 'What levels of craftsmanship are we being exposed to?' When I review theatre, I always take into consideration whether

I'm seeing professional, student, community, Broadway, touring, etc. I've had one of my most memorable nights of theatre seeing Shakespeare in a park in Winnipeg, and on the other side of the coin, I've experienced horrid, useless nights in some of the best theatres on Broadway. So, while budget and level of professionalism can shed light on the quality or standard one should expect, they are far from guarantees.

"I don't like a movie unless it has a happy ending."

"I hate films that are violent."

"I don't do war movies."

"I can't get into talking animals."

Sentiments like these are luxuries of consumers. When a person goes to the movies for his own amusement, he can remain as narrow-minded as he wants to be, but when you attend a screening as a critic, you have to see whatever your editor sends you to, or whatever you decide might be relevant to your readers. The best critics can appreciate a wide variety of cinema. Their tastes vary. They're able to shift gears, to adjust to the genre, the style and the spirit of what is projected on screen. That's not to say that a critic enjoys everything he sees, rather, it's *possible* for the critic to enjoy virtually any type of film. While it's realistic to have a beat at a newspaper or magazine that covers movies, it's absurd to say, "My beat is Westerns." It's a bit narrow and you won't wind up with many stories published.

Penelope Corcoran, dining critic for *The Arizona Republic*, began her career as a music critic. "In cutting my teeth as a music critic," she recalls, "I had to listen to tons of stuff – stuff that I hated, plus different styles of music I wasn't familiar with and had to bone up on.... Maybe country music isn't my thing, or maybe salsa music isn't my thing. But I can listen to it, and I can still figure out what is good about it, or what doesn't work about it. And maybe that's the mark of the ability to critique: the ability to step back from your own personal likes and dislikes, and say, 'This may not be my favorite kind of music or food or whatever, but they do it well.'" (5)

As a critic, set high standards that reflect your publication, readers and personal taste. Cover films that you, and/or your readers, will find important and/or interesting. But in the end, keep an open mind. Try to understand that while your personal experience with the film is deeply valid, your experience is not the only one, nor is it the definitive one. You are not bigger than the film. Craig Seligman argues this by urging, "Whatever else she brings into her writing, the critic has to keep her gaze focused on the work of art, and this willingness to place one's talent, one's ego, at the service of the artwork is central to any decent criticism."(6) Give every film a fair chance to succeed, fail, or most likely, do a little bit of both. In my life as a critic, I'm not sure that I've ever seen a film that is flawless, or one that is totally without merit. Usually, the best films have a chink in their armor somewhere, and the worst films might have one or two elements where they succeed. Look for those moments, those exceptions and point them out to your readers. Former *New York Times* critic, Janet Maslin (one of my all time favorites), wrote in a promotional piece published by the paper, "...even if a movie is awful, it's apt to be awful for an interesting reason."(7) Maslin isn't suggesting that we go soft on bad films. She's merely asking us to keep an open mind, to be absolutely fair and not to paint with broad strokes, if you will.

Pauline Kael also suggested that critics keep an open mind, but came from a slightly different angle when she said, "I don't trust critics who say they care only for the highest and the best; it's an inhuman position, and I don't believe them." (8) The implication here is that there can be merit and achievement behind arguably low-brow films like *Dodgeball, Wayne's World* or the *Austin Powers* series. A film doesn't need to be *Citizen Kane* in order to be considered a success. Kael is also suggesting that films with 'lesser' stars or smaller budgets can still be outstanding cinema.

Broadway Producer Manny Azenberg told Morely Safer on *60 Minutes* in March of 1991 that he felt critics should understand that producers take on projects because they see merit in them. He wants critics to consider what qualities the producers liked about the project, not just what the critic personally felt about it. In reference to the show *Einstein and the Polar Bear*, that *New York Times'* theater critic Frank Rich panned, Azenberg said, "Do you really think I produced it because I hated it? It's like telling you that your wife is ugly. *You married that woman? Are you crazy?* Nobody does that."(9) While Azenberg makes an interesting point, he might also consider that people don't usually charge $100 a seat to view one's spouse.

Occasionally, try to expose your readers to movies that they haven't heard of; that haven't been hyped and teased before their release. It's wonderful when you can uncover a cinematic jewel for moviegoers.

Continuing on with the problem of what makes a good film good or a bad film bad, let's partially deconstruct the elements of a production that one might conceivably comment on in a review. Certainly, not every element that we list will be mentioned in every review, but it is important to recognize, at least in part, some of the diverse components that come together in a film. If the list looks somewhat daunting and you begin to wonder, "How can I consider all these things and still watch the movie?" don't worry. After you write a few reviews, much of this will happen naturally in your mind as the film unfolds on the screen. Like most things, the more you do it, the easier it gets. Also, keep in mind that you're writing opinion. If you have good reasons for your thoughts and they're based on a solid cinematic foundation, it's difficult to be flat out wrong. Francois Truffaut points out, "We must not make exaggerated demands on critics, and particularly we must not expect that criticism can function as an exact science. Art is not scientific; why should criticism be?" (10)

Critics, like most journalists, wrestle with the demands of objectivity everyday. Advice that legendary CBS newsperson Edward R. Murrow offered his audience half a century ago still rings true for those who not only cover breaking news, but for those who cover film as well.

> "We shall make an effort to be as objective as we can. At the same time, we are fully conscious that there is no such thing as a wholly objective reporter. We are all prisoners of our own experience, of our reading, of our indoctrination, and our travels. We will undertake to give you as fully and impartially as we can the news from week to week." (11)

The Elements

Acting: Perhaps the most obvious element, it's difficult to overrate the importance of acting. One of the first questions asked by readers often is, "Who's in that movie?" or "How good was she?" Many times acting is not only part of the review, it winds up being lead material. Wouldn't most reviews of *Rainman* (1988) mention Dustin Hoffman and Tom Cruise in the lead? Wouldn't most reviews of *Sophie's Choice* (1982) mention Meryl Streep?

Acting, however, goes well beyond the leads. Very often the best performances in a film are done by supporting players, one reason why the Academy Awards recognizes their contributions. It's not uncommon to see a film with rather dull leading actors, that still manages an exceptional performance from a supporting player. Whenever warranted, give these people some ink. While I found Wynnona Ryder wonderful in *Girl Interrupted* (1999), Angelina Jolie was outstanding and worth a rave in any review that I'd write. And why not mention her in the lead? Years later, if you wanted to interview her for *Tomb Raider 7*, you could show her people your *Girl Interrupted* review and say,

"When others weren't sure how good she was, I made her my lead. I knew she was great the first time I covered her. Can I get 10 minutes to ask a few questions?" You might get lucky.

Supporting roles become even more important in ensemble films, where several actors all share screen time and lines; for example, *The Big Chill* (1983). Also, Woody Allen productions are often laced with talented performers who shine in their own roles, but like a great point guard on a basketball team, elevate the games of those around them.

That brings us to chemistry. Performers usually cannot be judged in a vacuum, as if what they do on screen is only about them. Many times it's a combination of actors that can make or break a film. The success of a film can be gambled on the chemistry between two actors. Did Michael Douglas and Glenn Close have chemistry in *Fatal Attraction* (1987)? Did Cary Grant and Kathyrn Hepburn have chemistry in *The Philadelphia Story* (1940)? Did Brad Pitt and Angelina Jolie have chemistry in *Mr. & Mrs. Smith* (2005)? Did Heath Ledger and Jake Gyllenhaal have chemistry in *Brokeback Mountain* (2005)?

Chemistry should not merely be limited to romance. Did Paul Newman and Robert Redford have chemistry in *Butch Cassidy and the Sundance Kid* (1969)? I'm sure studio executives and filmmakers expected Susan Sarandon and Geena Davis to have chemistry in *Thelma and Louise* (1991) Did Naomi Watts and Kong have chemistry in *King Kong* (2006)? Did Keir Dullea and the computer HAL have chemistry in *2001: A Space Odyssey* (1968)? Did Henry Thomas and the alien have chemistry in *E. T. The Extra-Terrestrial* (1982)? The interaction, or lack of, between performers can play a large role in a critic's review.

Keep an eye out for cameos. Famous people sometimes make very brief appearances on screen, perhaps playing themselves or some other character. Many times they make a single comment or have no lines at all. Alfred Hitchcock made a habit of getting in front of the camera for cameo shots in his films. The director even managed to get on screen in his 1944 classic, *Lifeboat*. Although almost the entire story took place on a lifeboat at sea, featuring several survivors of a U-boat attack, Hitchcock had his picture printed on a newspaper as the before and after client of Reduco weight loss program, so that it could be shown on screen while one of the actors in the boat, William Bendix, read the paper. (12) Not always worth mentioning in print, cameos can test a critic's eye.

Casting: The mandate here for a critic is to decide how well the actor chosen fits the role. Does Sylvester Stallone seem like a boxer in *Rocky* (1976)? Does Andie MacDowell sound like an English aristocrat as Miss Jane Porter in *Greystoke* (1984)? Actually, she does, but that's because Glenn Close was brought in to dub all her lines. Rumor has it that MacDowell's natural Texan accent was so overpowering, the English accent wasn't happening. In my mind, that's an example of being miscast. When Anthony Lane reviewed Ben Affleck's portrayal of Rafe in *Pearl Harbor* (2001) for *The New Yorker*, he said with tongue in cheek, "...his accent takes a patriotic tour of several states."(13) In other words, Lane believes that Affleck was likely miscast.

Another way to decide whether someone was miscast or not is to look at how they physically fit the role they've been asked to play. Pauline Kael began her review of *Top Gun* (1986) in *The New Yorker* by writing, "The strapping Kelly McGillis... the relatively diminutive Tom Cruise."(14) Kael seems to think that it's problematic for a largish woman to appear on screen with a smallish man. And so, they are in some measure miscast. Be careful here. Not only does Kael appear sizeist, isn't it possible, especially in the military, that a larger than average woman might fall for a "relatively diminutive" male, and vice versa? What's more important is, does their size detract from the ability to perform the roles?

If you want to use physical attributes to evaluate casting, a good place to go is athletics. Does Robert DeNiro look like a boxer in *Raging Bull* (1980)? Does Robby Benson look like a college basketball player in *One on One* (1977)? Do Ben Cross and Ian Charleson look like Olympic runners in *Chariots of Fire* (1981)? Does Hilary Swank seem like she can throw a punch in *Million Dollar Baby* (2004)? The next step would be to evaluate the way the actor moves. Does the performer appear as if he's ever skated before, ever taken a jump-shot, ever run around the block? It's not easy to fake athletic ability.

Does Ray Allen look like a basketball player in Spike Lee's *He Got Game* (1998)? Well, he should. Allen's been a perennial NBA All-Star. In this case, the public would want to know if the hooper can act (his performance was a swish, nothing but net).

You can also apply some of the same standards to music, westerns and dance. Does Geoffrey Rush look like he knows his way around a keyboard in *Shine* (1996)? In *Red River* (1948) does John Wayne look like he's handled a gun before? In *Chicago* (2002), do Rene Zelwegger, Catherine Zeta-Jones and Richard Gere look like they've danced before? Does Ed Harris appear to be comfortable with a paintbrush as Jackson Pollock in *Pollock* (2000)? Does John Malkovich look like himself in Spike Jonze's *Being John Malkovich* (1999)?... (This time, I'm kidding.)

At this point, there are probably readers who are scratching their heads saying, "Yes, this all makes sense, but really don't these judgements just boil down to individual taste?" Sure, there's plenty of gray area here, but what is your taste based on? Where does it come from? What are your expectations, your standards? How demanding are you? At the very least, I expect the film to be worth $10 and three hours of my time. That seems to be what the average viewer is asked to invest, so it's fair to hold the film to that standard. But being a critic requires making judgements that aren't painted with such broad strokes. Critics comment on a variety of diverse disciplines in the course of covering a film, so you need to cultivate taste in many different areas.

John Simon comes at the question from another, very useful angle in *Singularities*. He writes, "The man who spits at Praxiteles' Venus is really spitting in his own face. The beauty and nobility of the statue, which does not spit back, remain unimpugned.... True artistic talent is a marvelously unimpeachable thing..."(15)

Direction: In the evaluation of a film, the director can be as important as any actor. Certainly, names like Hitchcock, Huston, Fellini, Ford, Kubrick, Spielberg, Lucas, Allen, Scorsese, Coppola, Howard and a host of others all demand attention. They are the stuff of leads. It would be difficult to review *Goodfellas* (1990) without mentioning Martin Scorsese up front or *The Seven Samurai* (1954) without mentioning Akira Kurosawa.

Traditionally, if you have to credit or blame one person for the success or failure of a film, the director usually becomes the focus. While it's an overstatement, a film can really be labeled as the vision of the director. Do actors, writers, designers and others also bring their visions to the screen? Absolutely. But most often, it is the director who is credited with controlling the overall vision of the final product.

One of the reasons heavyweight directors are so recognizable can be traced to Francois Truffaut's groundbreaking article, "Une certaine tendance du cinema francais" (Cahiers du Cinema, January 1954). Commonly referred to as 'auteur theory,' the essence of the idea is that there is one person responsible for the content and style of a film. (16) While it's almost always the director, others, such as influential writers, producers, performers, editors, cinematographers and the like might be described as auteurs or artists within their own milieu.

Auteurs have a body of work behind them that features recurring themes, perspectives, styles and techniques that are displayed with some consistency. They generally function within the studio system and would not typically fall under the heading 'film artists'. To evaluate a director as an auteur is to take a holistic look at the person's entire body of work. What does it reveal about their method of personal expression on the screen?

Let's look at Woody Allen as an example of an auteur. He has a body of work and functions within the studio system. Before even walking into the theater, what could a critic guess she'd find on screen when reviewing one of his films? The film would likely be set in New York (London lately, for financial reasons, I'm told), feature big-name talent in an ensemble cast, look at some aspects of urban Jewish culture, examine marital relationships, feature characters in analysis, use adult humor, utilize jazz music, etc. One could go on and on describing elements that have appeared over and over in Allen's previous work. The same could be done for Quentin Tarantino, Spike Lee and a host of other filmmakers who, arguably, could be considered auteurs.

Beginning critics often underestimate the contributions that directors make and should not allow themselves to be mesmerized by acting alone. You should never write a review that doesn't give ink to the director.

Writing: Another element that should not be overlooked is writing. While being recognized at the Oscars, Steven Spielberg asked where all the great writers were, clearly suggesting that the foundation of great cinema lies with great writing. Also, the first question many moviegoers have when someone tosses a film title at them is, "What's it about?" They want to know the story. Likewise, when an actor, an agent or a producer is going to be pitched a script, their first question is usually, "What's it about?"

Remember that you're a reporter, a journalist commenting on the film being screened. Provide readers with the 5w's of the film's story early on in the review. Let them know *where* we are, *what* is happening, *who* is involved and *when* the film takes

29

place. (Yes, for those of you who counted, I know that's only four of the five w's. *Why/How* will be discussed at your discretion, because I know you don't want to 'tell me the ending' or give too much away.) Once the relevant w's are covered, you can move on to discuss the finer points of the production.

Jon Parales, music critic for *The New York Times*, makes an interesting observation that gets beyond the traditional 5w's. Even though he covers music, his thoughts are absolutely relevant for film critics. He says, "Don't tell anybody, but I think I have the best job at the paper. I get to go hear a lot of music. I get to listen to a lot of records and I get to think about it and tell people about it.... The *Times* lets me write about ideas.... A good newspaper should... tell people, here's what's coming out of the culture. Here's what seems to be on people's minds."(17) Just as Parales interprets the music he listens to, so should the critic reflect upon and interpret the films she screens.

While it's possible for weak performers to pull off a wonderful story, it's very difficult for wonderful actors to pull off a weak story. And, when we discuss writing and performing together, it's important to question what the actors were given to work with. Is it a good story? Does it shackle the actors or inspire them?

Stories can be generated from a variety of origins. They can come from original material; an idea that is written for the screen and has not previously appeared in other mediums. Stories are commonly adapted from literature and theatre. How many Stephen King or Shakespeare films have we seen? Stories for the screen have come from poems and songs as well. *Gunga Din* (1939) was adapted from a Rudyard Kipling poem. Folksinger Arlo Guthrie's popular song led to the satirical melodrama, *Alice's Restaurant* (1969).

Mel Brooks' *The Producers* (1968) began as a film about a show, then it became a show and has once again returned as a film, *The Producers* (2006).

When a film is adapted from a literary work, should the critic read the work? If your deadline permits and you judge the literature to be 'important' on some level to your readers and your analysis of the film, by all means. You don't want to be in a situation where thousands (or even millions!) of your readers might have read Woodward and Bernstein's *All the President's Men*, Michael Crichton's *Jurassic Park*, Stephen King's *The Shining*, John Grisham's *The Firm* or C. S. Lewis' *The Chronicles of Narnia*, but you didn't. Do you really want your readers better informed than you? If that were the case, why would they need to read you? On another level, how enlightening will your review be if you don't know how the filmmakers changed the story? Without reading the book you can't tell if a character was removed or an ending was changed. Those changes often represent comments from the director and others that will be lost on you. How will you be able to decide whether the film was true to its roots? Read the book. As the old public service campaign once said, "Reading is fundamental."

Stories have also emerged from TV shows and comic book characters. *Star Trek*, *Superman*, *Spiderman* and *Batman,* are very successful examples. *Wayne's World* (1992), *Blues Brothers* (1980), *Coneheads* (1993) and several other films were spawned from skits on television's *Saturday Night Live*.

There's no shortage of films that grew out of historical text or research, as well as newspaper stories, diaries, letters and other methods of recording events. The origin of a film's story can be of paramount importance. You often need to do more than just view the film to understand it. Do your homework, too.

While an individual script might be original, the concept of the film might not be. Critics review sequels, prequels and remakes, among other things. How many James Bond films have we seen? *Star Wars: The Phantom Menace* (1999) is sequencially a prequel, since the story takes place before the first three episodes released by George Lucas. *The Front Page* (1931), based on the Ben Hecht and Charles MacArthur play, has been remade at least four other times: *His Girl Friday* (1940), *The Front Page* (1949 &

1974) and *Switching Channels* (1988). Should a critic be aware of earlier versions and prequels? If you accept the argument that a critic should read the book, then wouldn't the same line of reasoning hold true for these situations?

Beyond the category of story, critics should also consider script and screenplay. The script usually focuses on the dialogue, the lines spoken on screen. Keep in mind that not every line spoken on screen is originally part of the script. Very often comedians; like Robin Williams, Eddie Murphy, Jim Carrey, Bill Murray, Vince Vaughn and others improvise on the set. Their work can actually make a script look better than it really is. Dramatic actors do this as well.

The screenplay includes the dialogue, but also incorporates camera techniques, effects, and other production values. It tends to be the most comprehensive version of the film in print. So writing is not merely limited to the story.

Some films present the story out of chronological sequence. Films like *Pulp Fiction* (1994), *Go* (1999), *Vanilla Sky* (2001), *Memento* (2000) and others use non linear sequence, at times combined with parallel plot construction to tell the story. That added dimension, or distortion, if you will, can sometimes make a story more interesting, or so convoluted that it's difficult to understand. I found the latter to be the case with *Syriana* (2005). It was a daringly ambitious film, but ultimately, less would have been more.

Many films begin by showing viewers a major plot moment and then taking the next 90 minutes to show us what led up to the opening scene. *Stand By Me* (1986) and *Inside Man* (2006) are examples. Be aware of the different storytelling techniques.

Within the overall story of the film, critics need to identify sub-plots. Stories that have depth, usually contain plot lines or strands that come together to create a bigger, more complete picture. But a sub-plot can also be misplaced and become a distraction. How many times have you seen a film fall apart because someone jammed a love story into the script? Must the anthropologist really fall in love with the native woman? However, be prepared for sub-plots that emerge as more interesting than the main storyline. Identify them just as you would a solid supporting player.

There's an old saying in Hollywood, "If you want to send a message, call Western Union." What that suggests is that movies don't send messages to viewers, that it's all just mindless entertainment. If movies are a form of communication, then they must have messages. Is there really no message in *Fatal Attraction* (1987)? And I guess *Meet John Doe* (1941), *It's a Wonderful Life* (1946), *The Last Temptation of Christ* (1988), *Turtle Diary* (1985), *Dr. Strangelove* (1963), *Dances With Wolves* (1990), *The Insider* (1999), *Twelve Angry Men* (1957), *Amistad* (1997), *The Killing Fields* (1984), *Schindler's List* (1993) *Fahrenheit 911* (2004), *Good Night and Good Luck* (2005) ... or even *Star Wars* (1977) send no messages to viewers... Really? If films are incapable of persuading viewers, why, since the beginning of their history, would they have been used as propaganda in cultures spanning the globe?

Films attempt to tell us what is good & bad, right & wrong, in or out, acceptable or unacceptable. The day after a film called *Flashdance* (1983) premiered, people all over the United States began tearing out the collars and cutting down the sleeves of their sweatshirts and slipping on leg-warmers. Why? Actress Jennifer Beals did it in the movie and it looked good on her. Tom Cruise looked so good flying a jet in *Top Gun* (1986) that recruitment into the Air Force and Navy pilot programs boomed. People actually joined the armed forces, during a time when the country was not at war, after seeing a movie. How many people walked around saying (President Ronald Regan included), "Go ahead, make my day," after seeing Clint Eastwood in *Dirty Harry* (1971) or "Show me the money," after hearing Rod Tidwell (Cuba Gooding Jr.) in *Jerry Maguire* (1996)? Wouldn't you have voted for Pedro at the conclusion of *Napoleon Dynomite* (2004)?

If you don't believe that films can tell us what to do and that Hollywood, in fact, believes that films don't send messages, then why would companies like Set Resources and others who broker deals for the paid placement of products into film projects, exist? Why would Reese's Pieces *buy* screen time in *E.T.* (1982)? Why would Pepsi, Taco Bell, Volvo and countless other companies pay to have their products seen on screen? Because the message generally is, if it's seen on screen, and better yet, used by stars, it's good. But in the same breath, Hollywood executives will tell you that there's absolutely no correlation between on screen violence and violence in moviegoers. How can a film encourage people to enlist in the Air Force; sell candy, cars, sunglasses and tacos, but *not* violence? Why would the effect suddenly and abruptly end there? When a 5th grader in an elementary school organized his own 'fight club' (which he created as a gang so he could bully other students) after seeing the film *Fight Club* (1999), how can anyone deny the cause and effect, even if it is anecdotal? While most certainly there are contributing factors and *Fight Club* is not rated for 5th grade consumption, this child still saw the film and formed a 'fight club'. That's not influence? And it doesn't end with children.

In *Behind the Screens: Hollywood Goes Hypercommercial* (2001) Susan Douglas, of the University of Michigan, points out that after the release of *Dirty Harry* (1971) viewers were moved to purchase a featured handgun, the .44 Magnum. She says, "This was a gun that was not selling particularly well, but after the film *Dirty Harry* came out the sales went through the roof." Professor Douglas feels it helped establish that, "... A movie could actually be an incredibly effective vehicle for selling a product."(18) Indeed, even a violent one.

In the same documentary, Robert W. McChesney, of the University of Illinois finds, "The line between the creative side and the business side of making films has been eroded. It almost doesn't exist anymore."(19) Professor McChesney warns that good scripts that don't have the potential to sell products will become less likely to be produced. And weaker scripts that can sell products will have a better chance of being made. For example, *Space Jam* (1996) gets green lighted, but Warren Beatty has to make *Bullworth* (1998) and Mel Gibson has to make *The Passion* (2004) with their own money. Ironically, all three films were financial home runs.

Critics don't just write about plots and acting; they interpret films. They ask questions. They delve deeper. And this is how a critic might look at messages in film. It's one of the ethics, this refusal to check your brains at the door, that makes you worth reading. "In 1958," Roger Ebert recalls, "I saw *Citizen Kane* for the first time and understood two things; that a movie could suggest the truth about a human life and that movies were the expression of the vision of those who made them."(20) (Disclosure: I had a similar experience some 20 years later as an undergraduate when I saw *Citizen Kane* for the first time.) Whenever you're covering a film, whatever the picture might be, try to identify the visions of those filmmakers. It's at the heart of any good review.

Films are packed with themes and messages, both overt and covert. They attempt to tell us what to think, what to say, how to dress, how to live, how to feel, how to react; and now more than ever, how to spend your money. Part of the critic's job (perhaps the most important job) is to identify and interpret these messages. What does this film say about being human, even if it's *March of the Penguins* (2005), because they all say something. Of less importance is judging the message. I personally believe, probably due to my journalistic roots, that readers and/or viewers are capable of judging for themselves. I try to communicate what I've seen and often how it made *me* feel, but I try not to tell others how they should feel. If life as a journalist has taught me anything, it's showed me how wrong I can be. So, try not to be too arrogant or sit too tall on the proverbial high horse (remember, the higher you sit, the further you can fall).

A closing thought on messages comes from *The New York Times'* George Amberg who maintains, "It is possible, in fact likely, that we still underestimate the social and cultural impact of the movies, their pervasive and inescapable influence in forming our notion of... man and his world. ...we have become accustomed to rely on information once removed from actuality and often removed from truth... any film is implicitly an *interpreted* version of the human scene, revealing graphically how people see themselves or, more significantly, how they wish to be seen."(21) It is vital that critics consider those "social and cultural" impacts. And, bowing to a basic ethic of journalism concerning the value of primary sources, critics must never forget that what they're seeing on the screen is, at best, a *representation* of truth, an "interpreted vision".

Editing: Commonly overlooked by beginning critics, editing is one of the most important elements of a film. For me, if I were writing a review for *The Hours* (2002), Peter Boyle's editing would be lead material. It was, perhaps, the most stunning aspect of that very fine film.

In many ways, the editing dictates the flow of the scenes and the pace of the picture. Just as passing the ball in a basketball game moves the action across the court; inside, outside, baseline, etc., editing moves the action on the screen, both point guards and editors set up the big shots.

If bad acting and bad writing can cause a film to drag, so can poor editing. Poor editing can also lead to confusion with respect to plot and story line. Conversely, crisp, competent editing combined with good acting and writing can make a three-hour film seem like it flew by in 25 minutes. On a smaller scale, editing can be a main ingredient in a memorable scene. Let's look at Alfred Hitchcock's *Psycho* (1960) for a moment. The most memorable scene in the movie (perhaps in all of Hitchcock's films) is the famous shower scene. That 45 second scene reportedly took one week to shoot, employed 73 camera placements, contains 57 edits and wound up becoming the signature scene of the film. In a 25 second span, there were reportedly 34 separate shots. (22) The film would never have been so memorable without the attention Hitchcock paid to editing.

In *Jurassic Park* (1993), a warden releasing a dinosaur gets dragged into the crate and is killed. The scene runs 2 ½ minutes and contains 43 shots, resulting in an average length of 3 seconds per shot. (23)

On the other extreme, it is the lack of traditional editing; the entire 2 hour-plus film is presented in one, running shot, that makes *The Russian Ark* (2002) such an incredible experience. Extremes usually demand attention and/or ink.

Cinematography: Just as vital as editing, or any of the elements of film, is the camera. While many viewers have become accustomed to the standard 'two shot' of sit-coms and other television productions, film critics need to pay attention to what the camera is doing. Placement, movement and effects should all be considered. When the camera was placed on the floor of Christy Brown's flat in *My Left Foot* (1989), the viewer was able to see the world from the same angle young Christy saw life. That placement provided perspective on the character, the scenes and on the rest of the story. The same thing happens when Martin Scorsese slowly lifts his camera to the ceiling, looking down at a bloodied Travis Bickle (Robert DeNiro) toward the conclusion of *Taxi Driver* (1976).

Traditionally the person credited (or blamed) for the use of the camera in a production would be the cinematographer. And, as we've said before, one could also include the director. Along with the director, the cinematographer designs the shots, chooses the lens, places the cameras, moves them and decides whether the camera will be hand-held, mounted on a tripod, a dolly, or a steadicam.

Pay attention to the camera. Does it look like we're watching a television sit-com, as if the camera was nailed into the floor, or is the camera alive? Are the shots creative? Do they speak to us? Do they enhance the film, the story, its characters? Occasionally you'll see a film where you could turn the sound off, sit back and just bask in the beauty of the images on the screen. I felt that way about Vilmos Zsigmond's work in both *The Deer Hunter* (1978) and *Heaven's Gate* (1980). When you see cinematography like that, give a little ink to the cinematographer.

Special Effects: With respect to special effects the scope is rather broad. Effects can be used with the camera, sound, editing, lighting, make-up, computer graphics (cg's) and in other ways. Keep an eye out for creative effects. Some can be very subtle. Often the best effects are not exploding Death Stars, but rather quiet backgrounds in diminutive settings.

Entire films can be built around effects. When I first began reviewing films, make-up artists were using something called a 'shape-shifter'. It enabled them to stretch latex masks and body parts. As a result, films like *An American Werewolf in London* (1981), *Wolfen* (1981) and *The Howling* (1981) were produced. Really, the effect spawned the movie. More recently, films like *Toy Story* (1995), *Finding Nemo* (2003) and *The Day After Tomorrow* (2004) could not be made without computer generated graphics. So sometimes, the effects are arguably the most important element of the film and can certainly wind up as lead material in your review. There are some critics who, with tongue in cheek, claimed that the mechanical shark in *Jaws* (1975) should have been nominated for an Oscar.

A word of warning, however. Be careful not to assume that all special effects are as obvious as Fourth of July fireworks. Some of the best special effects or computer generated graphics you'll ever see are created to look so natural that viewers never realize they're effects. Films like *Titanic* (1997), *Twister* (1996), *Gladiator* (2000), *Saving Private Ryan* (1998), the *Lord of the Rings* trilogy (2001 - 03) and the *Harry Potter* movies are chock full of examples.

Production Design/Set Design: For our purposes, production design will take into account set, props, costumes and all the little 'gingerbread' that finishes off the film. The costumes in *The Last Emperor* (1987), *Star Trek* (1979) or *Chicago* (2002) for instance, should not be ignored. They play an enormous role in making the film believable, and help the actors create their illusions. The same can be said for make-up and lighting. Some people believe, like a great umpire in a baseball game, if lighting and costumes are good, they will pass unnoticed. That's partially true. Certain productions call for these elements to blend gracefully into the fabric of the film. Others, like *Blade Runner* (1982) or *The Flintstones* (1994) call for costumes, lighting, set design, etc. to play a more conspicuous role. For me, the films that really set the bar with respect to both blending quietly and overt ostentation are the *Harry Potter* films. The production values in that series is unsurpassed in modern film. It's up to the critic to decide what role these elements play in a production and then assess whether they work or not. If you see something special on screen, give the people behind the props their 'props'.

Setting: Critics should pay attention to settings and always inform the readers, usually up front in the review blended into plot synopsis, just where and when the film takes place. Let readers know if they're seeing a period piece, set in a specific time and/or place [ie: *A Room With a View* (1986), *Gladiator* (2000), *The Patriot* (2000), *Troy* (2004) or *Capote* (2005)]. Once you've identified the setting, the next step is to decide two things. 1) Is the depiction accurate? 2) As is often the case in Shakespearean productions, was the time period selected a good choice? For example, was New York in the 1950's a good setting for *West Side Story's* (1961) depiction of *Romeo and Juliet*?

Another way critics uncover extra information about a setting is to carefully watch the credits. At times you'll find that Harvard was used to depict Oxford or that the Mohave was meant to be the Sahara. In *I Know What You Did Last Summer* (1997), the film opens with a shot of an oceanfront highway that runs along the 'winding cliffs' of... North Carolina? I've been to North Carolina many times and I've never seen mountainous cliffs alongside the ocean. Could the budget-conscious filmmakers have shot the scene on the Pacific Coast Highway, assuming that we'd all be too dense to notice? Critics should notice.

Sound: Don't underestimate sound. Much of the success of the opening scenes of *Saving Private Ryan* (1998) or *Star Wars III: Return of the Sith* (2005) is due to great sound. And, if great sound can help a picture, poor sound can hurt. Many times lines are lost, important ones, due to bad technique. Sometimes the sounds are recorded well, but mixed poorly. Crowds, music, wind, traffic and other noise in a scene can unintentionally overpower dialogue. If you're losing lines because the sound isn't mixed well, that's a problem. Levels can change too. I've seen films on tape and DVD where I have to change the volume from one scene to the next. That seems like a problem to me.

The theater itself can affect the sound as well. I try not to hold it against a film if the *theater* has a bad sound system. Effects like Dolby, Surround Sound, and other technical enhancements can also play a part in a film's success or failure. So, sound is a very important element, not to be ignored or underestimated.

Music/Soundtrack: Another element that demands attention is the music. How often does someone leave the theatre humming the theme song? Music can also be used as an effect: remember the moments before Jaws was about to strike? Daaa-dummmp, daaa-dummmp, daa-dummmp... with the tempo picking up as the carnivore creeps closer. The goose-bumps (or should I say shark-bumps) set in before the creature even appears on screen, thanks to the music.

A tune can become synonymous with a film. The theme for *The Godfather* (1972) is unmistakable. The same is true for the *Star Wars* and *Superman* series of films. Keep an ear tuned to the music. You might just be listening to what will become a signature piece.

Soundtracks can be noteworthy. While many are instantly forgettable, others take on a life of their own and can out earn the box-office. I'll bet that Jimmy Cliff's soundtrack from *The Harder They Come* (1972) generated several times the money the film has. The money generated by the soundtrack for *Saturday Night Fever* (1977) brought in more money than many other *movies* that year. The same is true for the soundtracks from *Grease* (1978), *Pink Floyd – The Wall* (1982), Titanic (1997) and others.

Keep in mind that an important part of watching a film, is listening to it. Pay attention to soundtracks, scores, musical effects and original music.

In the course of covering a film you will consider all of these different elements. Some will be more striking than others, while some elements won't be mentioned at all. The film, and your experience with it, will decide what makes the cut of your copy and how prominently it's featured.

The next two pages offer a basic list of the elements for consideration.

Basic Film Elements for Consideration

Studio:

Producer:

Director:

Actors:

       Leads:

       Supports:

       Cameos:

       Casting:

       Chemistry:

Story:

       Story by:

       Script:

       Screenplay:

       Plot:

       Subplots:

       Settings:

       Characters:

       Themes/Messages:

Original material or adapted from, based upon, inspired by:

       Book   Play   History   Song   Poem

       Television   Legend

Prequel or Sequel or Remake:

Cinematography:

    Cameras:

    Effects:

    Placement:

    Movement:

Editing:

Lighting:

Special Effects:

Make-up:

Costumes:

Set Design:

Production Design:

Sound:

Music:

    Soundtrack:

    Score:

    Effects:

Credits & Titles:

Budget:

Genre:

Place in History of Cinema:

Rating:

Runtime:

Chapter 2

Structuring the Review

"...instead of indulging passions in criticism,
one must at least try to be critical with some
purpose.... What is interesting is not pronouncing
a film good or bad, but explaining why." (1)

Francois Truffaut

There is certainly no one way to review a film. Different critics have different styles, many of them equally effective. In addition, the films themselves will affect your style. A comedy, for instance, might dictate a certain tone that wouldn't be appropriate for another film. Reviewing *The Passion* (2004) or any of the *Austin Powers* films would likely call for two different styles of writing. Films will generate varying levels of excitement, the amount of space an editor allows often changes and there will be other variables that will impact the way in which you write the review. That's good. The process should be alive. The writing should be alive. You don't want your style to become stale or cookie-cutter.

With that in mind, what follows is a very basic approach that should be helpful to beginning critics. Look at it as a roadmap, something to help you navigate the steps of producing a review. Those who have written a stack of reviews will probably already have an idea of what their own method and style is, or as John Simon refers to it, your "stageside manner."(2)

Let's assume two basic things from the start. One, you're writing for a general interest consumer magazine or a family newspaper. Two, your readers haven't seen the film yet. That hearkens back to the title, *Don't Tell Me the Ending!* Try not to reveal important plot lines or moments of resolution if you can help it. (This will be discussed in greater detail later in the chapter.)

Step 1) The Lead

Like any journalistic story, the review needs a lead. Keep in mind that this beginning paragraph is arguably the most valuable real estate in the story. This is where the reader will decide, in a matter of seconds, whether to continue reading or look for another article. My advice is to begin your review with a little pizzazz. Give serious thought as to what might be lead material, and conversely, what can come later on in the review. Only the most relevant/interesting material is worthy of the lead. You can tell us the running time and rating later.

Probably the simplest approach is to begin with the *names*. Usually that means star performers and/or directors. It's difficult to review *My Left Foot* (1989), for instance, without naming Daniel Day-Lewis up front. How do you review *Patton* (1970) or *One Flew Over the Cuckoo's Nest* (1975) without mentioning George C. Scott and Jack Nicholson in the lead? Would you cover *Monster* (2003) without mentioning Charlize Theron or *Hurricane* (1999) without mentioning Denzel Washington? These actors are lead material, because in many ways, they are the film.

Big names often call for big ink. But actors aren't the only ones with recognizable names. Directors can also be featured in the lead. It is possible that a relatively unknown director (or actor) could become lead material due to his or her achievement on screen (or perhaps due to a remarkable lack of achievement). Bennett Miller when he made *Capote* (2005), or Quentin Tarantino when he made *Pulp Fiction* (1994), or Stephen Spielberg when he made *Jaws* (1975), or Spike Lee when he made *Do the Right Thing*

(1989) all serve as examples of young directors who distinguished themselves. However, a director is usually noted because he or she has a name that readers will recognize. Names like Kubrick, Hitchcock, Allen, Speilberg, Lucas, Scorsese, Copolla and many others are commonly cast in the lead paragraph.

Beyond performers and directors, writers and producers are sometimes lead material. Neil Simon, Stephen King, John Grisham, J. K. Rowling, Jane Austin, Lillian Hellman and many other writers are often deemed lead material. Usually, a writer surfaces in the lead when she or he has authored the book or the play the film is based on. There are also many legendary producers in Hollywood. And sometimes, a big name producer hires an unknown director in order to maintain control on a film. In those instances, the producer might be more newsworthy than the director. There are also those people who have made names for themselves on both sides of the camera; as actor-director and/or writer-producer. Woody Allen, Clint Eastwood, Mel Gibson, Spike Lee, Kevin Smith, Jodie Foster, Robert Redford, Warren Beatty and others are all multi-talented, multi-faceted filmmakers/actors.

One can also produce a solid lead by turning to the film itself. The 'situational lead' begins by bringing the reader into the movie. It tells the reader where we are and what we're faced with in the film. In a review I wrote for *Biloxi Blues* I used the situational lead...

> *It's 1943 and six young soldiers are being sent to Biloxi, Mississippi to begin basic training. They'll learn more about themselves and their friends than about killing the enemy.*(3)

Another way to approach the lead is to use a quote from the film. For a *Forrest Gump* (1994) review, you might begin with something like...

If *'life is like a box of chocolates'*... then so is the film, *Forrest Gump*; a sweet surprise in every bite, given to the audience with the innocent sincerity of someone offering a box of confections to a loved one. And like that gift, the film is memorable, touching, and very satisfying.

You can begin a review using a quote from someplace other than the film. When I reviewed the Frances Ford Copolla resurrection of Abel Gance's *Napoleon* (1927) that was presented in Radio City Music Hall in 1980, I began with a quote from the band Steely Dan...

I have never met Napoleon but I plan to find the time.
Cause he looks so fine upon that hill.
They tell me he was lonely, he's lonely still.
Those days are gone forever, over a long time ago. (4)

I followed up the quote with (whenever you use a quote, whether it's from the film or not, always try to tie it to the movie or some observation) a suggestion that *Napoleon*'s days aren't over by a long shot, and that with all the people piling into Radio City Music Hall, he can also forget about being lonely.

For a magazine story I wrote for *Inside Books Magazine* in 1988 about the *Star Trek* book series, I began by doctoring the famous quote that introduced each TV episode... "Space, the final frontier. This is the story of the starship Enterprise. Its mission: to explore strange new worlds, to seek out new life, to boldly go where no man has gone before..."

Space, on store-front tiers. This is the voyage of the Star Trek book series. Its mercantile mission; to explore strange new characters, to seek out new plots and new readers, to bi-monthly go where no book series has gone before. (5)

Another way to approach the lead might be from a thematic angle. After watching *Fatal Attraction* (1987) one might begin... *Fatal Attraction will do more to generate fidelity among couples than any disease or divorce settlement ever could. I dare you to cheat on your spouse after watching this film.*

Don't be afraid to be creative. But keep in mind, if your idea works, you're a genius. If it doesn't, then you should have known better. You will always be second-guessed by those in charge, so take your chances, but think them through.

Some general thoughts about the lead: Try not to say too much. Try not to do too much. The lead should happen quickly. Simple tends to be better. Don't forget, you have the entire body of the review to accomplish whatever you can't get done in the lead, so if it's not of vital importance, do it further down in the review.

Also, beware of Hollywood buzz. Often it's spawned from publicity people who have vested interests in the film's success. The 'buzz' is commonly clothed in fabrication, hyperbole and sensationalism, none of which are admirable journalistic qualities. In this sense, the critic needs to be a filter. Don't allow yourself to be distracted. Over time, the court of public opinion will decide whether the buzz is warranted and whether it will stick. In the meantime, it's usually better to concern yourself with what's on screen. The rest will sort itself out later.

Lastly, whatever form your lead takes, try to give readers an indication as to how you feel about the film. Set the tone for what will follow in the rest of the review and let them know, right out of the blocks, if this is going to be a 'love-in' or a 'slam-fest'... or something in-between.

Now that you've written your lead and provided an indication as to whether you enjoyed the film, a good way to figure out what to do next is to look at what questions your readers will typically ask first. In my experience, when I tell someone I've seen a movie (or read a book, or seen a show) one of the first questions I'm usually faced with is, "What was it about?" So, why not start there? Do you really want to discuss acting, or messages, or production values *before* you tell readers what the film's about? Couldn't that be confusing?

Follow up your lead with some brief plot synopsis. How brief? Well, there are two things to consider here. First, let the film itself decide how much space you need to use. I would think *Caddyshack (1980)* and *The Godfather* (1972) call for differing amounts of plot synopsis. One might take a paragraph or two, the other might call for several paragraphs. Next, consider what you're going to reveal. I assume (and not all critics do) that my readers haven't seen the film yet. And so, for me, the golden rule is *DON'T TELL ME THE ENDING!* Why should I tell potential viewers whether Bill Murray gets the gopher in *Caddyshack* or whether Michael whacks Fredo in *The Godfather*? One reason I don't read reviews, or watch trailers, before I see a film is because they tend to give too much away. If I know that 'David builds the time machine' or 'Sarah animates the cartoon series' or 'Randi gets on the Springsteen tour bus;' when it happens on screen the effect will be diminished.

In her review of *Raging Bull* (1980), Pauline Kael (whom I have tremendous respect for... I use *For Keeps* as a text in my own Film Reviewing class) writes, "When he [Jake LaMotta] loses the title and gives up fighting, he opens a night club, where he's the m.c. and the comic." Later she adds, "The Mafia bosses force Jake to throw a fight before they'll let him have a chance at the title. He throws the fight by just standing still and taking the blows; afterwards, he weeps."(6) Why do I need to know all that? Could reading that before I go to *Raging Bull* diminish the experience for me? Of course it will.

The tension over whether Jake will win the title or throw the fight is gone. The curiosity over what he'll do afterwards is gone. And even though the film is based on a true story, that doesn't mean most of the viewers know the story. So why would you reveal major plot points when you know the film will?

Be careful when you discuss, not only the ending, but also subplots. Try to talk *about* the film without *telling* the film. This is one of the most difficult things for a critic to do. You need to be both specific and vague at the same time. Journalists often decide to write something, or leave it out... all or nothing. Going halfway, or part way can run against the grain of common practice. Writing 'vaguely specific' or 'specifically vague' also violates one of the most basic journalistic credos, to always be as specific as possible, but good critics who truly are concerned with their readers' experience in the cinema must make the attempt. No one enjoys the loudmouth who exits the theater telling everyone what just happened inside. Why would people feel differently when critics behave that way? Don't be the loudmouth leaving the theater in your review. There are many people who don't read reviews because critics "...give too much away."

If a plot line is resolved early on in the film, or the picture is built upon some important initial action or fact, and much of the ensuing film is constructed around this moment, it might be necessary to disclose the early event in order to discuss the plot. Usually, the later a plot line comes to fruition, the less likely you would reveal the result to your readers. If you do have to go there, try to employ some form of being vaguely specific.

An example of being vaguely specific might work like this. Rather than telling readers, "Mafia bosses force Jake to throw a fight... He throws the fight... afterward he weeps." Kael could just as easily have written, "Mafia bosses pressure Jake to throw a fight in order to get a title shot. Faced with one of the toughest decisions in his life, the boxer must weigh advancing his career against sacrificing his integrity in the ring, probably the two most important things in Jake's life. Whatever he chooses, it's a decision he'll have to live with... if the mob lets him."

The difference between this passage and Kael's original is that now there's a level of doubt. As a reader, I know *specifically* what choices Jake is faced with, but it's still *vague* as to what he decides. This is an example of being vaguely specific. I get to do my job as a critic and still protect the readers' enjoyment of the film.

As a critic, anytime you find yourself writing phrases like; *She comes to believe..., In the end..., He realizes that...* take a step back and ask yourself if you're giving too much away. Perhaps there's a way to make your point and still leave the plot line unresolved for potential viewers.

When covering the plot, don't be afraid to mention sub-plots if they seem relevant. Also, let readers know something about where the film goes. What countries do we visit? What period does it cover? Set the table. Identify the genre of the film. Is it a western, a dark comedy, noir, fantasy, romance, historical or some combination of genres? Also, it is sometimes a good idea to mention the writers here. Crediting or blaming those who wrote the story/screenplay can fit nicely with plot. It's usually effective to keep *like* things together. This will reduce both reader confusion and the *tennis-match effect*; where readers bounce back and forth from one unconnected idea to the next. The rule here is; start it and finish it. Then move on to something else and do the same.

Now that you've covered the plot and your readers have a good sense of what the film is about, most people tend to wonder how the big name talent performed. This is a good time to evaluate the acting and/or other notables whom readers will be wondering about. What did they achieve? What didn't they achieve? And, to what degree did these things happen? Try to support your claims by asking yourself, Why did I say that? I've always felt that the most valid opinions are based in fact and that the least valid facts are built on opinions. Whenever you can, lay your opinions upon a foundation of facts.

There are times when you'll blend some of your evaluation of the performers into the copy covering plot. When you mention a character in plot synopsis, sometimes it's a good idea to evaluate them briefly right there. Likewise, when you make your first reference to a character, try to tell readers who played the role. For example, if you were reviewing Tim Burton's *Edward Scissorhands* (1990) and mentioned the title character, on first reference you would write: 'Edward Scissorhands (Johnny Depp)' or 'Edward Scissorhands, played by Johnny Depp'. If you choose the latter, try to add some indication of how he performed. For example, 'played a cut above by Johnny Depp' or 'played sharply by Johnny Depp' (in both cases, the lame pun is intended).

After the lead, plot synopsis and acting, it's not a bad idea to address production values. This is where you can get into the nuts and bolts of the film, the mechanics of the movie. Everything from set design to soundtrack, from make-up to editing can be examined. If an element doesn't warrant mention, leave it out. There's no rule that demands that every review evaluate in print the lighting techniques used. Mention only what strikes you. Try to connect names to elements. Who did the lighting? Who did the make-up? Credit or blame actual people whenever possible. In this context, you are looking at their performances. That edit is part of the editor's performance. Those shadows are part of the lighting director's performance. Every element, judged in its own milieu, represents as much of a performance on behalf of its craftsperson as any actor takes on.

The next step would take us away from production values, lean closer to story and serve as a vehicle to bring us in the direction of the closing. Discuss with the readers what the film is about in a larger sense. What morals or ethics does the film profess? What does the movie tell us to do, to avoid? How does it suggest we should behave? What are the themes? Oliver Stone's *Wall Street* (1987) brings to mind the signature quote, "Greed is good." Is it? Is that the message of the film? Or, is Stone really saying something else? In Paddy Chayefsky's/ Sidney Lumet's *Network* (1976) the signature quote is, "I'm mad as hell and I'm not gonna take it anymore." Have a good ear. See if you can hear and identify if there will be a phrase that people will associate with the film. Remember, by the time everyone is saying, "Do behaaave...," like Austin Powers, you will have already written your review, so you need to be a cinematic psychic of sorts. Getting back to *Network*'s "I'm mad as hell...," tell readers what this means and how it relates to the overall message of the film. Just as movies have several plot-lines, they also tend to send several messages. Without giving too much away, identify the more striking ones for your readers. Occasionally, the message might even become the lead.

Don't be afraid to compare the film to other films. Remember, you're writing to people who speak movies, so give them movies. When writers pitch ideas to producers they often phrase their treatment by saying something like, "It's *The Little Mermaid* meets *Titanic*" or "It's Darth Vader goes to college; *Star Wars* meets *Animal House*." I write a series of environmental novels and often describe them to people by saying, "They're like *Finding Nemo* meets *March of the Penguins*. It's okay to discuss the story and its characters in terms of other films and their characters. Critics occasionally compare films to TV shows, paintings, plays and other examples drawn from the arts.

Somewhere around this time, I might make some general comments about problems with the production. If there's major mistakes, nodding to the inverted pyramid, I would probably do that higher up in the review. Lesser problems or concerns usually fit nicely into this section of the review. For example, I found the music in *A Knight's Tale* (2001), a medieval movie with serfs nodding stiffly to Queen's "We Will Rock You" at a joust, absurd. It's not lead material and it's not something I'd like to leave out, so towards the end, after the heavy lifting is done, is often a good spot to mention it. When you do make a point, whether negative or positive, try to be quick about it. Less is more. Don't belabor the point and don't be redundant. Say it once, clearly and move on. (After all, it's a review, not a film textbook.)

Although it's sometimes lead material, toward the end of the review can be a good spot to discuss just where the film figures historically. Has it achieved something or discussed something that hasn't been touched upon before, or perhaps something that has been examined ad-nauseam? Is it a first, or even a rarity? Where does this film stand with respect to others from the genre? Those comments, if appropriate and not earth-shattering, often fit nicely toward the end of the review.

Now it's time to start thinking about the closing. There are several things to accomplish here. I sometimes begin these closing paragraphs with warnings and/or advice for the readers. One area that could require a word or two of warning is the rating. I try to tell readers how appropriate I feel the rating is. And, perhaps why the film received its *R* rating. Was it for language, nudity, violence, drug use, sexual themes or some combination of these things? Was the ratings commission accurate? Do you agree with what they've decided? Is there something that I should explain to my readers about the violence, the language or the nudity?

Another situation that might call for a warning is when you address who should or shouldn't see the film, something I usually do towards the end of the review. First, a word about assessing the likely audience: Is it a 'think piece', a 'good cry', a 'chick flick', a 'guy movie', a 'dating film', a 'check your brains at the door' picture, etc.? Without being overly offensive or insensitive, sexist, ageist, etc., give readers an indication whom the film will likely work for. 'For fans of Mel Gibson *The Year of Living Dangerously* (1983) is a must-see.' 'If you're hooked on hoops, add two more stars to *Hoop Dreams* (1994).' 'If you read Stephen King and were disappointed by other adaptations of his work, you'll love *Misery* (1990).'

If it's appropriate, you might also point out who should stay away from the film, or who might be offended by the picture. For example, after I saw *Saving Private Ryan* (1998), I wondered whether I should recommend the movie to my dad. You see, my father served in World War II in an amphibious assault unit. While I found the film an incredible experience and believed my father would too, I suspected that for many people who actually lived through the events depicted on screen, they should understand what was coming before they entered the theater. So, in a review of *Saving Private Ryan*, one might point out that people who are normally moved by the violence of war films; people who either lived through, served in or lost a loved one in WWII; and veterans in general should understand that Speilberg's film, especially the opening 20 minutes, will transport you back in time to the beaches of Normandy, France. You will be shot at, you will see death and you will get a sense, as remote as it might be, of what it was like to stare into the guns of the Nazi's as you and your comrades stormed (and in many cases, died on) the beach. If you're not prepared to return to the battle on the beach, you might want to avoid this film.

In closing your review, give readers a very concise idea of just how good, or bad, the film is. You never want someone to read one of your reviews and then say, scratching his head, so did she like it or not? It can be helpful to provide an indication of whether the film is any good or not in your lead, but in your closing you should state what you think, leaving absolutely no doubt where you stand on the matter. Do you recommend the film? How strongly, and if you haven't done it already, to whom? Will it win awards? How many stars does it deserve? This summation will give the reader a sense of closure. The most basic decision many readers make when they finish reading a review is whether they should see the film, so this is a good spot to unambiguously address that question.

Lastly, I try to end the review with a little pizzazz. Just as the film needs to entertain the viewer, *you* need to entertain the reader. In fact, you need to entertain, these days especially, just as much as you need to inform. The better critics are able to accomplish both, often at the same time. If someone is going to endure my discussion of the merits and faults of a film, then they deserve a little something for the effort. I try to make the ending as special, as well crafted, as the lead. Film Scholar David Bordwell of the University of Wisconsin, writes, "The best reviewers excel as writers. They render their opinions in short, memorable strokes. They devise arresting openings and pointed wrap-ups." (7)

There's another reason why I believe the closing is so important; one that Professor Bordwell would likely agree with, the theory of Primacy versus Recency. What's more important to a reader: the first thing they see or the last thing? In other words, what's more important; the lead or the close? It's usually during the lead that people decide whether they will keep reading. If they don't get past the lead, they'll never get to the closing. The lead is the 'first impression', and you know how important it is to make a good first impression. When you make a bad impression right out of the blocks it can be almost impossible to undo. So obviously, the lead is vital to the success of the review.

But the idea of *Recency,* 'What have you done for me lately?' is also important. And the close, which leaves the last impression, can be what readers ultimately take with them when they are done reading. If the closing is weak, all that wonderful work that preceded it might be forgotten, or at least diminished. So, the closing is also vital.

Which one is more important? I have no idea. It depends on the reader, the writer and the film. However, what I do know is that they're each significant. I advise that you hedge your bets and make sure both the lead and the close are given the attention they deserve. Give your readers a special lead *and* a special close. They'll look to read you more often and your editor will give you more opportunity.

There are a few final thoughts I'd like to share on the actual writing of the review.

First, try not to contradict yourself. Take a stand and stay there. In her review of *Saturday Night Fever* (1977) for *The New Yorker,* Pauline Kael wrote, "These are among the most hypnotically beautiful pop dance scenes ever filmed." That would appear to be a rather large statement (although I wonder how many 'pop' dance scenes were filmed prior to *SNF*). Yet when Kael discusses the two main dancers in the film, John Travolta and Karen Lynn Gorney, in the same review, she writes, "Travolta doesn't appear to be a 'natural' dancer..." and " Gorney isn't much of a dancer."(8) Well if the two main dancers are so obviously flawed, how can their pop dance scenes be among the best *ever* filmed? While in another part of her review Kael does point out that Travolta successfully *"acts"* like a dancer (which clearly suggests that he's not *a dancer*), her criticisms still seem to fly in the face of her praise. The lesson here is to be consistent with whatever you profess.

Following the notion of being consistent, another thought comes to mind. Try not to over-enthuse or make use of hyperbole. Guard your credibility. Don't buy into the hype. Early in my career, when I reviewed Abel Gance's restored *Napoleon* (1927/1980), I used several phrases like; "...one of the most amazing scenes I have ever seen in all of film," "I can't think of an improvement he could have made," and "Some of the best child acting I have ever seen...."(9) These are HUGE statements. They should not be made lightly. If you throw them around from review to review, ultimately your credibility will suffer, and when you find that phrases like these actually apply to films, the impact, after repeated use, will be subverted. So, try not to over-enthuse. In retrospect, looking back at my clumsy review, I realize why I wrote what I wrote. Part of it was perhaps due to the hype; Radio City Music Hall, Francis and Carmine Coppola, a live orchestra, an artifact being restored and re-released, etc. But really, I did feel what I wrote. I was honest. I did see "the best child acting," "the most amazing scenes" and I couldn't "think of an improvement" ...because I was naïve. I hadn't seen or studied enough films, hadn't written enough reviews at age 20 to have the proper perspective to make statements like that with credibility. So, in the end, my motives were honest, but my experience was too thin.

Returning to Kael's review of *Saturday Night Fever*, she writes about John Travolta, "It's getting to be a joke – another Italian-American star."(10) Is there really some limit on how many performers we can have from a specific heritage? How many black actors are too many? How many Jewish actors are too many? How many English actors are too many? Are there too many men? Are there too many women? For a critic to single out Italians and claim that there are enough, more than enough, in fact, is absurd. Can you really have too many DeNiro's, Pacino's Brando's or Travolta's for that matter? Would she claim that there are also too many Italian directors? Perhaps we have enough films from Scorsese, Coppola, Fellini, Minelli and others. Personally, I try to judge people on ability rather than by how many vowels are in someone's name. Having an actor with an Italian background play a young man from Brooklyn who has a brother who's a priest, who likes to eat pizza and disco dance makes sense to me. As a critic, always question your biases. Comments like Kael's don't tend to increase credibility.

While I'm regularly in awe of Kael's insight and perception, I'm also often amazed at her tendency to miss the central point. In her review of *The Little Mermaid*, she wrote, "Parents seem desperate for harmless family entertainment. Probably they don't mind the movie's being vapid, because the whole family can share it, and no one is offended."(11) Although Kael is generally on target with her observation, she couches it as a problem. Let's table the debate over whether the film is 'vapid' for now. As a critic, as a parent, my question is, what's wrong with 'harmless family entertainment?' And, what's wrong with no one being 'offended' with a children's film? In my mind, these are strengths, not weaknesses. As a critic, your personal opinion is extremely valid, but try not to lose sight of how movies will play to other audiences.

One thought I'd like to re-emphasize is the value of statement and support. Don't assume that readers will know what you mean or that they'll agree with you. It's safer to generally assume the opposite. When you say that someone was miscast explain why. Give us an example, if you can, of who might've fit the part better. The idea is that you'll *show* the reader, rather than *tell* the reader. Although it's not always possible to do so, wouldn't it be more powerful for someone to read your comments, your reasons, and then say to you, "It sounds like she was miscast." Whenever possible, allow your readers to see what led you to your conclusion, support the statement.

Try to make your copy as clean as you possibly can: Mistakes matter. They have a direct affect on your credibility as a critic. The more mistakes you have in your copy, the more mistakes you're likely to have in other areas of your work. That's the equation editors and readers generally subscribe to.

I wrote a story for an entertainment magazine as a favor to a friend. I was asked to cover films being released for the winter holiday season. Among the films I wrote about was Francis Ford Coppola's *The Godfather; Part III* (1990). I submitted my copy, squeaky clean, on deadline and the magazine published it as the lead story of the entertainment section. When I read the published piece, I found NINE typos that weren't in my original manuscript. The editor actually spelled Coppola with a 'K'. I had hoped to use the piece as a vehicle to land other assignments, but after the 'Koppola' disaster, I couldn't show it to anyone. When I questioned the editor, she replied that she 'spell-checked the story,' as if that's all an editor needs to do.

But beginning writers can be just as unprofessional. Don't hand in copy that's partially done. Don't give the editor six inches when she asked for ten. If you can't write to count, then a little more is always better than a little less. It's easier for editors to trim copy, much harder to expand copy. And it's *your* job to finish the story, not the editor's. Don't expect them to complete your assignment. If you do, you'll be working on holidays and writing about little things that get buried deep inside the publication. Even though your best efforts can sometimes be thwarted by a poor editor; as a professional you should always give your best.

Here's a framework for the basic review that you just read about. Remember, you're not locked into anything. This is just a guideline to help you get started and to keep you focused. Use it as a roadmap to help find your way through those first few reviews. However, don't cling so tightly to this that you hinder the development of your own style. A detour here and there might not be such a bad thing.

LEAD : Potential Material

- *big names*; star-power (these could be directors, writers and others beyond the actors).
- *situational*; a taste of the action
- *direct quote*; either from the film, from another film, or from music, politics, etc.
- *news*; budget, firings, injuries, break-ups, arrests, suits, etc.
- *historical*; 'never before'...
- any combination of the above
- some wonderful invention of your own
- remember to indicate whether the film succeeds or fails
- give readers a taste of the tone that will follow in the body of the review
- practice the five B's (be brief, brother, be brief)

PLOT SYNOPSIS :

- Don't overdo it, but give us a good sense of where we are and what's going on. Remember the five W's.

PERFORMANCES :

☞ Start with the leads, but don't ignore noteworthy supports and cameos.

THEMES & MESSAGES :

☞ What does the film tell us about ourselves? What does it endorse? What does it condemn? Identify and interpret as needed.

☞ Keep in mind that the last three categories can be combined. It's possible to cover all three, more or less, together.

PRODUCTION VALUES :

☞ Occasionally you'll do it higher up in the copy for more effect-laden films, lavish period pieces and others.

☞ You're looking more at the mechanics of the film here.

HISTORY & GENRE :

☞ What genre (if any) does this picture belong to?

☞ Where does this production place in relationship to other similar films?

CAUTIONS, CONCLUSIONS & ENDORSEMENTS :

☞ Does the rating need elaboration?

☞ Who should or shouldn't see this film?

☞ Begin to set up your closing.

CLOSING :

☞ Make it special. Give it a little style, a little pizzazz.

☞ Leave no doubt in the reader's mind where you stand on the film.

Chapter 3

Covering the film.

"... stature as a critic has... to do with... intelligence, knowledge, experience, sensitivity, perceptions, fervor, imagination, dedication, lucidity – the traditional qualities associated with great critics. The role of the critic is to help people see what is in the work, what is in it that shouldn't be, what is not in it that could be. He is a good critic if he helps people understand more about the work than they could see for themselves; he is a great critic, if by his understanding and feeling for the work, by his passion, he can excite people so that they want to experience more of the art that is there, waiting to be seized. He is not necessarily a bad critic if he makes errors in judgment. (Infallible taste is inconceivable; what could it be measured against?) He is a bad critic if he does not awaken the curiosity, enlarge the interests and understanding of his audience. The art of the critic is to transmit his knowledge of and enthusiasm for art to others. (1)

Pauline Kael, from *I Lost It at the Movies*

Please find your seats. The feature is about to begin.

Screenings are a funny thing. Just like films, they come in all shapes and sizes. I've attended screenings for 1,500 people and I've attended screenings for a dozen people. The first screening I ever went to was in Manhattan for the film *Heavy Metal*

(1980). I was a critic on my college newspaper, double majoring in English and Film. A friend of mine, John Caragiulo, worked for the company that did titles for the film and he had an extra pass to the screening. He offered it to me. After the screening we were all invited to go to a party celebrating the film. Buses waited for us outside the lavish New York theater. Being a typical college student of the times, I climbed onto the bus and never asked where it was going. The fact that there would be a party when the doors opened was all I needed to know.

When the doors finally did open we were parked in front of the Guggenheim Art Museum. The museum was closed, unless of course you attended the screening. As my friend and I entered the main hall, we saw food, drink and a band on a small makeshift stage in the center of the floor. Surrounded by world class works of art, critics and filmmakers, Cheap Trick played, and played, and played. I stayed until they 'asked' us to leave. Exiting the Guggenheim with no hope of catching the last train out of Penn Station, I turned to John and said, "This is too much fun. I have to be a critic!"

But one of the things you learn early on is that as much fun as it is covering film, when you enter the theater, you're on the clock. In other words, you're working. Don't be swayed by the studio-generated ballyhoo. Don't get too caught up in the *side*show. The show the critic should be mainly concerned with takes place *on* the screen, not around it. Try to focus on the job at hand.

Getting Started

How does one get into a screening? There are many ways, but for critics you generally need to have a solid publication behind you. The word 'solid' will be defined by the people putting the screening together. Some studios will be satisfied by smaller weekly and daily newspapers (college newspapers, too... hint!), while others will invite only major daily newspapers and important monthly and weekly magazines. There are variables that come into play.

When I covered films on a daily basis some studios had 'A' 'B' and 'C' lists. The 'A' list critics were obviously invited to everything. (To rephrase the a popular adage: 'They'd be invited to the opening of an envelope.') 'B' list critics were 'tweeners. They went to most events, but might not make the cut of the most exclusive opportunities. And, 'C' list critics would usually be invited to screenings of films like *Sheena* (1984) or *Rustler's Rhapsody* (1985) (both of which I attended). An invite could also depend on where you worked, what you wrote perhaps, and/or the marketing strategy behind the film. For example; while your magazine might have a smaller circulation, its demographic could be a match for the target audience of the film. *Breaking Away* (1979) is being released and you write for *Bicycle Monthly Magazine.* That might get you invited. Perhaps the film premiering is not very good, but your publication has a history of printing favorable reviews. That could get you invited. Maybe you've networked yourself into the good graces of someone at the studio. That could get you invited. Both minor members of major publications and major members of minor publications can also wind up with access.

If you think you should be on the invite list and you're not, let the studio's publicity people know who you are, where you work and what you do. Call them and/or e-mail them. Send them several of your favorite reviews (it could help if one or two of their films are included, at least one of which you might've had some appreciation for). Send them a sample of the publication you write for. I suggest that you use e-mail initially, wait a week and then follow up with a phone call to 'confirm that they received your material'. Once you have a human being on the phone, you might be able to connect with him personally. That can help. But remember, these are busy professionals and you're one of many people vying for their attention. Most likely you're also a very small fish in their rather big pond, so always be patient and polite. Make it easy and nice for them to work with you and the odds increase that they will want to.

If you do get access and want it to continue, always send the PR people copies of reviews that you've written of their films. Thank them for their help (of course, without compromising your critical abilities). A sincere thank-you note to someone who helped you can pay huge dividends, keeping you placed favorably on their radar. Whenever I had extra tickets to screenings or concerts, I tried to share them with colleagues and others in the industry that remembered me when they had opportunity. I remember a record company receptionist calling to alert me that Annie Lennox (of the Eurythmics) was in the office and asked me if I wanted to do a quick exclusive interview with her. I did the interview. As a result, the record company, Lennox, my readers and I all benefited from that phone call. I made sure to thank that receptionist and remembered her when I had something that might interest her.

As a critic, you'll likely rub elbows with a host of Hollywood players of varying prominence. Always keep in the back of your mind that the biggest people don't always have the biggest stories. Very often the less noticeable people have wonderful information and might be more forthright in sharing it. That receptionist who booked your screening today might very well be the director of Public Relations a few years down the road. Try to play nice and appreciate everyone's effort, then they'll probably do the same for you.

The best reason to be invited to a screening, and the best way to get put on the 'A' list, is to work for a reputable publication where you produce fair, evenhanded reviews on a consistent basis. It's tough to argue with quality. That might also get you better assignments, promotions and more opportunity at other publications.

Almost every invite that I've received over the years read, "You and a guest are cordially invited to..." Should a critic bring a guest? Well, if you plan on covering the film, you might be better served to go solo. Perhaps you could invite one of your publication's editors (who might appreciate the night out) or photographers (who might score a few celebrity photos). If you do bring a guest, try to remember that you're working. Your attention should really be directed more toward the film than your companion or the event of the screening.

Distraction is a common problem at screenings. I've attended screenings where savvy studio public relations executives set up fabulous catered spreads, complete with wine, champagne and other temptations. Again, if you're covering the film, practice some modest restraint.

Here's an example of a young writer whose restraint was not nearly so modest. It was my first day on the job at *Modern Screen Magazine.* I was still loading supplies into my new desk when the editor came to me and apologized, saying that he had to send me out to cover an important screening even though I hadn't quite moved in yet. ABC had produced a TV movie, *The Day After* (1983). The film examined what it might be like the day after a nuclear holocaust. Word was that ABC had no sponsors, who feared the topic, but ABC was committed to airing the film, even without commercials if need be, primetime on a Sunday night. The network decided to have a press screening for all the New York based critics, hoping to generate some favorable press, preferably to be followed by a steady flow of advertising dollars.

I took a cab to the Plaza Hotel, where the movie theatre was reserved for *The Day After.* I walked through the door that morning, told the person in the ABC blazer my affiliation, happily accepted a thick press kit and several promotional trinkets and made my way into the Plaza. I was informed that there were still a few minutes before the show would start and was asked if I'd like a little breakfast. Thinking, *When in Rome...,* I said, "Okay." The breakfast that I received was nothing short of the Plaza's best. I'll never forget it. Manned by a dozen, uniformed chefs, everything from Eggs Benedict to Belgian Waffles were available. There were bagels and lox, donuts and strudel, assorted juices, champagne... even ice cream. I must admit, being new to the profession (it was my first day on the job!) I ate... a lot.

When the lights flickered I made my way to my seat, thrilled to be among so many recognizable film writers. But before the film began rolling, a man walked out in front of the screen, introduced himself as the director, Nicholas Meyer, and began answering our questions. POOF! Instant interview! Next, Jason Robards, who played Dr. Russell Oakes, walked out and did the same. I remember thinking how happy my editor would be when I returned with comments from the director and the star. Perhaps it would make a nice sidebar, I thought, as I scribbled feverishly, trying not to tip my plate over. (Yes, I brought a 'small' dish into the theater with me... Come on, we're talking PLAZA food!)

Then the movie began. It was a long film, around three hours if I remember correctly. When it was over I gathered up my press kit and other trinkets and prepared to get back to the office. However, when the house lights came on a woman from ABC invited us all to lunch in a private banquet hall upstairs in the hotel. Since it was lunchtime, and I was more or less still in Rome, I decided to accept the offer. Lunch turned out to be quite an affair; several courses, the main one being an unforgettable Marsala dish with succulent almond-topped green beans. We dined with a flock of ABC soap opera stars; two of whom, one female and one male, were strategically situated at each table. As they flitted from chair to chair, we chatted with them, scheduled a few for interviews and even posed for photos that ABC would 'messenger over to the office in case we wanted to run them in the magazine.'

By the time I got back to my office, at the close of my first day on the job, I was dizzy. As I sat at my new IBM Selectric typewriter ready to write my review, I looked back on the events of the screening. The taste of the mouthwatering Marsala lingered as I began to press the keys. A small satisfied smile creased my face. And then I wrote a rave about how wonderful *The Day After* was. I really felt that way. It was a controversial topic that demanded coverage and ABC had taken a brave stance declaring that they would air the film without commercials if need be. It was a very impressive production; television of the highest order. But I wonder, when they saw the piece at the network, did the PR people also smile a satisfied little smile and say, "It was the Marsala, gets 'em every time."

Before You Enter the Theater

There are a few things that you should think-about/take-care-of before you enter the theater to screen a film. Actually, there are a thousand things.

Personally, I try to come in with a blank slate (for me, that's pretty easy). Seriously though, I avoid reading other critics and I avoid watching trailers, whether they're on television or running prior to a feature in a theater.

I'm assuming that most people read me to see what *I* thought of the film. If they want to see what Roger Ebert thought, they'd read him, so I avoid looking at other critics' reviews before I've written mine. Sometimes you can't look at other critics' work because you've attended a press screening and no reviews have been written yet, or perhaps your deadline won't allow you to consult other reviews. You see the film and you file your review hours later, along with most everyone else. That happens more often in daily journalism. But when you write for a monthly, or even a weekly, you might have the opportunity to look at what other critics have written. For me, that's cheating. These should be your thoughts, totally. But not all critics agree. In her review of *The Little Mermaid*, published in *The New Yorker* on December 11, 1989, Pauline Kael wrote, "I didn't expect the new Disney *The Little Mermaid* to be Faust, but after reading the reviews ('everything an animated feature should be,' 'reclaims the movie house as a dream palace,' and so on)..."(2) Kael obviously looked at several reviews *before* she wrote her own. Not only that, she ran two quotes from other reviews and never cited whose words they were or where they appeared in print. Again, my advise is that you not look at other reviews about a film you're covering until after yours has been submitted.

I feel somewhat the same about watching previews. How can they possibly help you with your job? All they do is give you information about what will happen in the film before you should know it. Why do I want to know that Pacino gets shot? Why would I want to know that Foster finds her way home? When this finally happens on screen, the experience will be diminished because the preview will have impinged on the dramatic value. So, if a preview appears on the screen when I'm watching TV with my family, I'm one of those people who covers his ears, closes his eyes and sings some goofy song so I can't tell what's going on. (Yeah, I know, I could just hit the mute button on the remote, but my way is so much more fun.) My family really appreciates this, by the way.

The New Republic's Stanley Kauffmann has a deep appreciation for the possibilities of film; the idea that once the projector is fired up *anything* can happen. In *Why I'm Not Bored* he wrote, "No matter how much I know about a film's makers or its subject before I go, I never *really* know what it's going to do to me: depress me with its vileness, or just roll past, or change my life in some degree, or some combination of all three, or affect me in some new way that I cannot imagine."(3) It is precisely because of those awesome possibilities, in an effort to keep them pure, that I try to walk down the aisle, to some reasonable degree, with a blank slate.

When booking a screening, critics are usually invited to one of two showings; a 6:30pm and a 9:00pm for example. Typically, these screenings will take place on a Tuesday, Wednesday or Thursday evening, to allow time for the critics to place the review in the paper's Friday weekend edition. This timing can lead to bigger box office for the studio and a nice night out for the public, provided the film garners some good comments from the press. Whenever you see a film premiere without any press screenings, or if screenings take place on a Friday night, it's usually a safe bet that you'll be seeing a dud. When presented with the figure that from January to April in 2006, eleven films opened without being screened for the press (4), *The Wall Street Journal's* Joe Morgenstern said:

> "I'm not surprised that the studios are skipping critics screenings when some of these atrocities hit the screen. What is there for critics to say, except variations on the theme Arrrgh? The mystery is why they didn't start doing this several years ago?"
>
> [Publicists know] that many of their superiors would rather not show films to critics at all. Especially to print critics, who offer more potential loss than gain." (5)

As I said, if a film was released without a screening, or the screening was on a Friday night (which a decade or more ago was quite uncommon), I could safely guess that I was going to see a pretty weak production. The studio was dodging the critics in hopes of scoring a big opening weekend before the critics roasted the film and drove down ticket sales. But longtime *Asbury Park Press* movie writer Eleanor O'Sullivan recently identified a disturbing trend for critics. She wrote in her column, "...many movie companies will no longer routinely screen their movies in advance for critics' reviews."

She points out, "So-called 'event movies,' the big budget extravaganzas such as *Superman* and *Lord of the Rings*, will continue to be screened in advance, as well as art-house films that need the boost that comes from good reviews. It's the marginal, niche market (i.e., teenybopper) and sure duds (by critics' lights anyway) that will be increasingly kept away for fear of harsh criticism." (6)

When it comes to the time of the screening, I almost always choose the earlier screening. Not only does it get me home earlier and give me a bit more time to gather my thoughts, if I find myself confused by the film (what are the odds?) I can stay in my seat and catch a second showing. I did this in Los Angeles when I saw the premier of Peter Hyams/Arthur Clarke's *2010* (1984). When the film was over, I had no idea what I had just seen and how it related to *2001*, so I stuck around for the next screening. It helped.

It does, however, raise a question for the ethically minded critic. Is it right to see a film twice? If you don't quite 'get it' after one showing, shouldn't you just write about that? The rest of the public will probably not see the film twice, and your experience should ideally reflect theirs. So, staying for an extra showing is kind of cheating.

Pauline Kael would probably agree with that. In her Introduction to *For Keeps*, she says, "I wrote at first sight and, when referring to earlier work, from memory. This had an advantage: urgency, excitement. But it also led to my worst flaw as a writer: reckless excess, in both praise and damnation."(7) Kael seems to be suggesting that a second screening might actually temper and refine her judgement. While my staying for a second screening spawned an ethical dilemma for me, Kael's 'single screening and references based on memory' eliminated that quandary, but raised a professional concern of her own "reckless excess."

The one way to ethically deal with the 'second screening' dilemma, might be to disclose and discuss what happened to you. Let readers know that what follows is the result of a second showing, that after you initially saw the film you felt you needed to see it again. I find it's usually better to share things like this with readers. If, for instance, you were asked to review a western, and you don't like westerns, you might tell readers,

"I enjoy watching westerns about as much as I'd enjoy eating boiled tumbleweed." Then, at least the readers would know where you're coming from. It's honest. (By the way, I generally enjoy westerns and have never tried boiled tumbleweed.)

Before you sit down to see the film, try to have a decent meal and visit the bathroom. You don't want to get up and walk out of a film you're covering because you're hungry or nature calls. Keep in mind, your comfort can affect your attitude. To be fair to everyone, you don't want your attitude about other things to be unduly projected onto the screen and likewise into your review. It's not fair to place the burdens of stomach, bladder, mood and other variables onto the film. I've never seen a studio claim that a movie will nourish you or relieve you, so don't expect that.

While screening *Fahrenheit 9/11* (2004), I ran out of paper. Moments before I started writing on my arm, I realized that I had an extra pad tucked into the leather binder I use to record my notes. An extra pen and an extra pad can be lifesavers if you need them, so bring them along. They're not heavy. And as long as we're on the subject of *Lifesavers* , I like to keep a mint or two in my pocket. They can help you weather dry moments in longer films without leaving your seat.

When you choose your seat, keep a couple things in mind. Obviously, if you sit in the first few rows you'll be leaving the theater with your neck out of joint. You don't really need the film to happen in your lap. On the other hand, if you sit in the last few rows you might have a good idea of how the audience in front of you is responding, but the screen becomes so small you might as well be in your living room watching it on television. I like to sit in the middle rows, cheating toward the front. It leaves me with viewers between my seat and the screen, yet the film is still big. Let's face it, dimension is part of the theater experience. I want a massive picture and big sound. Beware the extremes; front, back and sides. If you have a bad seat, it might play a role in how you evaluate the film.

Don't be late. If I walk into a theater and the opening credits have begun for a film I'm writing about, I leave and come back to the next showing. And I absolutely never leave before the film is completely over. You can't cover something that you haven't seen in its entirety. To do so would, in my mind, be both unethical and unprofessional. Would you cover a baseball game having seen only five innings? Would you write about a CD having only listened to 'some' of the songs? In order to be fair to readers, filmmakers and your publication (not to mention yourself), you must see the entire film. How many times have we seen important plot points established in the first few seconds, or addressed in some snippet after the credits [*Finding Nemo* (2004) for example]? A good guideline for any journalist is to show up early and stay late.

I've seen many fine critics who watch films and then write reviews, never taking a single note. Roger Ebert is one of them. (8) I don't, albeit can't, work that way. I'm not saying I'm right and they're wrong. To each her own. What I will say is that I don't have enough good ideas that I can afford to lose any. I write them down. If I didn't, my reviews would always miss one or two points I wanted to make that escaped me when I sat at the keyboard. I take pages of notes.

For some, the writing will be distracting in the beginning, but you'll get used to it. When needed, I'll catch light from the screen to see what I'm writing. I've also seen people work with little light-up pens (generally frowned upon). You have to be respectful of other viewers, so forget the halogen. There have been times when I've written three sentences on top of each other and couldn't decipher a single word later on. I learned to write just a few comments spaced generously on a page and then move on to another page. Like most things, you'll figure out a system that works for you. Dr. David Bordwell would also appear to encourage note taking. He says, "Some people say that watching for [cinematic] techniques distracts them from the story, and it is true that many movies try not to call attention to their style. But you can learn to watch for both technique and story. It's multitasking, like driving a car while carrying on a conversation. It just takes practice." (9)

When you're taking notes, free associate, brainstorm, write whatever pops into your mind. Remember, you're just gathering thoughts. When you get back to your office you'll decide which ones to keep and which ones to toss. However, my advice is that you generally sketch your thoughts into your notes. I'll use one, two or three words written in 'moranohand,' my own version of shorthand, to record the idea. Don't sit there composing complete sentences while the film is passing you by. You don't want to spend any more time distracted, even momentarily, from the screen than you need to be. Afterwards, you'll take those thoughts and develop them into full-blown sentences and paragraphs.

I jot down impressions (*'reminds me of...'*), observations (*'great camera...'*) and general facts (*'lives in NY, works as a plumber...'*) from the story that I might use later. I also try to record several fun or exemplary direct quotes. They can really come in handy. In my review of *Mr. & Mrs. Smith* I was able to build my two final paragraphs around quotes:

> Having purchased gaudy new curtains for their upscale
> home in he suburbs, Jane advises John, "If you don't like
> them, you can take them back." Her husband replies, "I don't
> like them." Jane counters, "You'll get used to them." *Mr. &
> Mrs. Smith* fails, just like those gaudy green curtains. And while
> we can't return the film, let's at least not get used to it. Another
> 2-plus hours of beautiful people shooting at each other...please.
>
> When assassins have a domestic dispute, things can get
> explosive. John complains about his spouse using a tool of the

trade during an argument. Jane's response, "Oh, come on, it
was just a little bomb." I couldn't have said it better myself. (10)

Listen to the film. Make use of interesting quotes to further your review, giving it local color and a nice specific flavor. Many times the characters will say exactly what you'd like to say.

Pay attention to the audience. Director Steven Spielberg says, "If the audience likes it [the film] and you don't, they'll encourage you to see beyond your own prejudices and enjoy it more than you would if you saw it alone."(11) How are they responding? Do they get it? Are they laughing when they should be crying; moaning when they should be laughing? Are they restless? Is the theatre so quiet you could hear the proverbial 'pin drop'? I also listen to people chat as I leave the cinema. It's a habit I picked up covering theater. Whenever there was an intermission, I'd stand in the lobby with a beverage and listen to what the people were saying. Every now and then, I'd get a good idea for a line or a better sense of how the show was playing to other viewers. The same can happen as you leave the movie-theater. Critics are reporters, so don't be afraid to do a little reporting.

When the titles roll, I usually stay in my seat, look for interesting credits and try to gather my thoughts. How has this film made me feel? At the moment it's over, what am I thinking? Sometimes, this makes for interesting copy later on. Often, there are thoughts or feelings that you won't recall if you don't take a moment when the film is over and they're fresh in your mind.

One of the last things I do before I write the actual copy of the review is to organize my notes. Usually, I have about five or six pages of thoughts that I've scribbled onto my pad. There are always sentences and words that are difficult to decipher, so I take a few minutes to re-write all my notes. Since most of what I've written is just a brief sketch of what I really want to say, I take a moment to embellish, to develop the ideas. I try to re-organize them as well, taking like things and putting them together. I group thoughts about acting, direction, themes, etc. In working the notes, my thoughts become clearer and I get a better understanding of what I want the review to achieve. It's a very important part of the pre-draft process. Preliminary steps lead to drafts, which lead to the finished copy.

Putting Pen to Paper, or Fingers to Keyboard

Once your notes are sufficiently cleaned, it's time to start writing. Everyone has their own style, their own method, so I'll leave that to you. I don't expect my students to be me (I wouldn't wish that on anyone). The goal is to figure out who *you* are on the page. You're trying to find your voice. That can be an elusive pursuit, since as a writer you can change based on what film you're covering and how you grow as a person throughout your life. When I was single, living in Los Angeles and New York, I wrote differently than I did after I became a married professor. Now as a (gulp) middle-aged dad, my writing has evolved in others directions. Still, there are many traits that I developed as a student critic, that are with me today. Writing is not a stagnant thing. Just as you're alive, so should your craft be alive. We've all heard bands record the same song over and over, seen directors make the same film over and over, watched writers write the same story over and over. Try not to write the same review over and over. Mix it up. Keep it alive. Try different techniques.

You're writing to people who go to the movies. Use the language of the film, otherwise known as local color, to pepper your copy. When I covered the show *Biloxi Blues*, I wrote that the production featured "a platoon full of talent."(12) When I covered *Dodgeball* (2004) with Ben Stiller and Vince Vaughan, in my first draft (I did like the film) I wrote that it was "as predictable as a sunrise." I liked the phrase, but felt it was a little cliché and that I could make it better with some local color. Since the film is about competition between two gyms, I changed the phrase to "as predictable as a pull-up". (13) For me, that's a better line. It's specific to the film, has a touch of alliteration and still makes the point. Although it's a brief part of a longer review, as long as you don't over do it, there can be a cumulative effect. When you pay attention to those little details, your work will improve. And really, it's those little details that separate the professionals from the amateurs.

One way to improve your writing, perhaps the best way, is to write in drafts. When I was a youngster at basketball camp, I had a coach who wrote on my evaluation, "never be satisfied with good enough." For some reason, those words stuck with me, not only in sports, but also with regard to life in general. Apply them to your writing. Work the copy to make it better. Try to improve word choice. Try to clean up vague sentences. Eliminate unneeded words. In short, write in drafts and edit your copy to the best of your ability. Like most things, the more you do this, the better you'll get at it. Also, your editors at the publication you're writing for will appreciate the effort. It's a good idea to give them less work, not more. As a result, you'll find that fewer of your sentences have been changed. Your lead will get printed the way you wrote it. You'll wind up with a reputation as one of the 'clean' writers. You'll get better assignments and they'll break out the red pen for the person in the cubicle next to you. That's a good thing.

Write simply, clearly. This is *mass* communication. A large number of readers need to understand what you're saying on the first read. If they have to go back and try to figure out what you're saying, you've blown it. Don't be misled, very often it's the simplest writing that takes the most work.

Writer's block (also known as 'literary constipation') is not a luxury that critics can afford (science has yet to discover a literary laxative). Your review needs to be written when your editor wants it, not when it feels right for you. I've reviewed many shows that end at 10pm and my copy is expected at 12:30am. Those tight deadlines can be scary, but they're also kind of fun. The chief film critic for the *New York Times*, A. O. Scott, knows a lot about writing under deadline pressure. He points out:

> "You don't get to work on a piece for months, they are not
> going to run the movie for you seven times. [Your job is]
> not to get it absolutely right, but as right as you can...
>
> Any kind of writing has its constraints. What you write is
> disposable. What you write about is disposable. What you
> try is to take things as seriously as you can, to be as serious
> as you can, within the context of speed." (14)

While it is somewhat true that many films and many reviews, perhaps most even, are "disposable", I try not to look at it that way. One reason is that the label "disposable" is often assigned well after my review was filed, so I try to assume that both the film and my work are more or less keepers. For me, it just helps me work harder and take things more seriously. But the point Scott is really trying to make here, I believe, is one of paralysis. As a critic, you cannot be immobilized by the quest for perfection. You have to produce the best work you can in light of the situation you're faced with.

Personally, however, I always felt more comfortable writing for monthly magazines, where I often had the chance to let the film sit with me a few days before I had to file my story. On rare occasions, especially after a rushed deadline review, I would see the same film a second time after my initial story ran and feel a little differently about it. That's a bad feeling. [It happened to me recently with my review of *Cold Mountain* (2004).] But I don't recall ever re-writing an initial review or really having the opportunity to.

That's one difference between covering film and theater. Once you write a film review, once you've seen a film, that's pretty much it. Traditionally, there's no need to revisit [unless, of course, we're talking about a remake, for example, *The Manchurian Candidate* (1962 & 2004) , *The Longest Yard* (1974 & 2005) or *All the King's Men* (1949 & 2006)]. In situations like these, where there's 20, 30 or 40 years between remakes, you're looking at an almost entirely new cast, director and crew. It's really a different film. In theater, however, when a major cast member changes, when a show has been running for a long period of time, or when the director changes; a critic will often find her way back into the theater to produce another review.

Getting back to the notion of writers' block, one other thought comes to mind. If deadline permits, I like to chat with friends about the film, whether they've seen it or not. To be totally honest, on those rare moments when I can't find a human friend, I'll talk to my dog Max about the film. I find that the discussions help me organize my thoughts. They help me find ways to express what I'm thinking, what I'm feeling. And while I have no intention of writing their opinions (especially Max's), my part of the conversation functions like a draft of my review. Sometimes *saying* what you'd like to write is almost as good as writing it. That just might be the thing to get you past your writer's block. It's all about words being used to express ideas. If you can find the words to say what you mean, you're on your way to finding the words to write what you mean.

In *A Short Guide to Writing About Film* (2004), author Timothy Corrigan would seem to agree with the previous statement. He writes:

> Let us keep in mind that writing about the movies is
>
> not so far from what most of us do already: when we leave a
>
> movie theater after two hours of enforced silence, most of
>
> us discuss or argue about the film. Although the difference
>
> between talking and writing about a subject is a crucial one,

> writing about a film is in one sense simply a more refined
> and measured kind of communication, this time with a reader. (15)

Always keep in the back of your mind that whatever you write is, to paraphrase Pauline Kael, 'for keeps'. Once you've said it, there's no backing off. Here's an example of the first time I realized that. As an undergraduate at Clark University in Worcester, Massachusetts, I decided that I wanted to become a film critic. I promptly joined the school newspaper as one of their critics. Then I declared a double major in English (to learn story structure, characterization and to improve my writing) and Screen Studies (to learn the lingo, history and the elements of the industry). When it came time for my end of year 10 Best/10 Worst List, I came up with an idea. I decided that I'd select a very popular, big time film and include it on my 10 Worst List. I thought this might get people to read. And, as luck would have it, there was a film that the public loved, but I loathed. Satisfied that I would not be compromising my ethics (too much) I placed the film number 1 on the list.

The day the student newspaper, *The Scarlet*, hit the campus, I was walking back from Prof. Hodgekinson's British Cinema class when I heard someone call my name.

"John… John, can I talk to you for a moment?"

I turned and saw Prof. Ray Munro, Chair of the Theater Department, standing next to me. I had taken his class the semester before and had a lot of respect for him, to say the least.

When he had my attention, he continued, "I read your story in this week's paper and found it quite interesting."

"*Of course you did,*" I thought to myself, pleased that a professor of Munro's standing would take the time to read my words and consider my thoughts 'interesting'.

Then his expression changed. He looked at me as if he didn't really know me, asking, "Did you learn *anything* in my class?"

"What do you mean?" I asked.

"Did you learn anything?... I mean *French Lieutenant's Woman* as the *worst* film of the year. Really? Are you serious?"

Sensing an imminent lambasting from the eminent professor, I tried to back-peddle, saying, "Well, I didn't really say it was the *worst* film of the year."

Prof. Munro raised his index finger and said, "Oh, I think you did." Then he reached into his back pocket, removed a copy of the paper and read my own words back to me. There was no denying, no place to hide. I was pinned up against a tree and it was like the professor was beating me over the head with the rolled up newspaper. He wasn't, but that's what it felt like. At that moment, thanks to Prof. Munro (really), I learned that I would be held accountable for whatever words were printed with my by-line above them. That realization hasn't prevented me from writing controversial comments, but it has served as a litmus test to remind me to make sure I can defend whatever I write. By the way, *The French Lieutenant's Woman* (1981), which featured names like Streep, Irons, Pinter, was widely described as an intelligent, inventive success. I still don't like it.

Chapter 4

Film critics should go to the theater.

"A person not sensitive to sets—or costumes,
or lighting, or background music, or make-up,
or whatever else—is not likely to be all that
sensitive and tasteful about theater in the larger sense."

John Simon, *Singularities*:
Essays on the Theater 1964-1974 (1)

If you want to do a better job covering film, you should go to the theater. After all, they really are cousins. Many publications can't afford to have one person covering only film or only theater, so you should be prepared to cover either. One way to get prepared, is to do it. Whenever possible, I added theater classes to my schedule as a student and I attended plays on or off campus. This helped me understand the elements and nature of stage performance.

One of the first plays I covered in college, was *Amadeus* on Broadway. I drove down to New York City from Worcester, Massachusetts to cover the show. When it was over, I went backstage and interviewed the star, Peter Firth. A few years later, when I was an editor at *Modern Screen, Amadeus* the film won eight Oscars after being nominated in eleven categories. Having seen the show on Broadway, I had a valuable point of reference in understanding what the filmmakers had done with Peter Shaffer's play about Mozart and Salieri. Just as it can be vital for a critic to read the bestseller before writing the review, or screen the original before covering the re-make, or preview the prequel before attending the sequel; seeing (or reading) the play before it becomes a film adds perspective.

Critics understand that the budget often affects what's on screen. They take into account whether a film is Studio produced, Independent, Foreign, etc. The reason to do this is to establish levels and expectations. You want to judge the work through the appropriate set of lenses. That same ethic should also be applied to theater. Are you on Broadway? Have you pulled into a regional theater to see a traveling production? Is this an undergraduate presentation at the local university? Are you sitting in a folding chair in the all-purpose room of a neighbor's church? Each venue commands a different ticket price. Is it fair to expect that $5 in the collection plate should provide the same level of entertainment as $150 at the box office? Each venue suggests a different level of performance, but none of them are guarantees of anything. I've seen absolute garbage on Broadway. I've also had unforgettable experiences, at any price, covering student theater at Clark, Penn State and Monmouth Universities.

Have you ever seen a movie-in-the-round? Probably not, and you're not likely to unless you're in a planetarium somewhere. I have, however, seen several shows in-the-round. It can be an incredible experience. It also underscores the idea that the theater itself is often an important element in the production, something that is refreshingly anti-multiplex. Most theaters have their own personalities. While you would normally not comment on the acoustics or the ambiance of theater #12 at the local multiplex, these considerations are often worth a line or two in your theater reviews.

The playhouse is not the only thing alive in theater. I'll let you in on a little secret (only seasoned professionals know this). In theater, the people on stage are also alive. It's true! Those actors hear the cell phones ringing. They respond to laughter, applause and deafening silence. They show up and perform with fevers and sore throats. They make mistakes one night that don't happen the next night. Each performance of the play is unique. You won't find that in film.

While I was a graduate student at Penn State I earned extra money (as if there's such a thing as 'extra' money) covering theater and the arts for the Center Daily Times, the local Knight-Ridder daily serving central Pennsylvania. Due to a tight deadline at our paper, the publicity director of a campus production invited me to attend the final dress rehearsal to review the show. Not wanting them to lose out on the exposure the review would provide, I accepted the invitation. The review that I published, like the play, was mixed. The headline that an editor placed atop the story was slightly less 'mixed', but in my judgement, still fair. It read; *Thespians' 'Cabaret' a bit uneven.*(2) This moment raises two concerns. First, you always take your chances when you file a review and you leave it to an editor to come up with the header. While they know the layout and the space limitations, often editors don't fully read the copy or have a sense of what the critic has written. It can be a disaster when the headline and the copy are in conflict (although that wasn't the case here). The second concern comes with my reviewing a 'final dress rehearsal'. As primarily a film critic, I don't think I fully grasped the gravity of covering a rehearsal. I shouldn't have done it. But, at the same time, the show's publicity director never should have offered the opportunity. In film, while I've never covered a rehearsal, I have actually screened movies that were still in a rough cut stage. I screened *Teachers* (1984) as a rough cut, but again, was encouraged to do so by the studio. For me, looking back, the key is once again disclosure. If you're going to do it (and you probably shouldn't) at least explain the conditions under which you viewed the film/play to your readers.

Because theatrical productions are more 'alive' than film productions, critics will occasionally return to the theater to re-review a show if a new director takes over or if new performers step into major roles. That was the case when Nathan Lane and Matthew Broderick left their roles in *The Producers*. Along the same lines, every time you slip Mel Brooks' film *The Producers* (1968) into the DVD player, you will find Zero

Mostel playing opposite Gene Wilder... every time. But in a staged production, there's really never a guarantee that the stars will perform. Understudies step into the limelight and sometimes generate headlines in the world of theater, a phenomenon not really encountered in film, unless something similar happened on the set *before* the film was released.

The technique of acting can be different for performers on stage. Clint Eastwood's whisper and the Rock's raised eyebrow work wonderfully when their faces are 15 feet tall projected onto massive screens, but those same gestures would likely be lost to most of the audience if those actors relied on such subtle techniques on stage. This is one reason why you see so many performers overplay their parts in early films. These were usually theater people who had little experience in front of a camera. It took some time before filmmakers and performers appreciated how the camera would change the viewing experience for the audience. There's a belief among many entertainment professionals that suggests we've come full circle from the days of theatrical overacting. To paraphrase, it says that many screen actors can't really attempt serious stagecraft, but trained theatrical actors have no problem with film and television.

Make-up, lighting, costumes, blocking and especially set design, are potentially much more significant elements of theater coverage than film. History, particularly of roles and productions, generally plays a larger part in theatrical reviews. Because most productions are limited in their run and are performed by a single company on a single stage (more or less), for older more established plays there is usually a history behind them. Imagine how many interpretations of *Hamlet* there have been. While cinephiles might discuss the merits of the various 'Bonds' or 'Draculas,' there are many more examples of this phenomenon in theater.

Writers are historically given more prominence, credit and celebrity in theater than in film. Williams, O'Neill, Pinter, Chekov, Ibsen, Stoppard, Hellman, Shakespeare and too many others to list represent theatrical royalty, while screenwriters for movies largely remain anonymous to the general public. It's common to see shows billed as 'Peter Shaffer's *Amadeus*' or 'Tennessee Williams' *A Streetcar Named Desire*'. But when critics look at a filmed version of the material, it's usually discussed as 'Elia Kazan's *A Streetcar Named Desire*' or 'Milos Forman's *Amadeus*'. Although there are good reasons for both billings, critics should not underestimate the contributions that screenwriters, novelists and playwrites make to the productions they review. In a similar light, producers in theater tend to be given more regard than directors, while in film the opposite is generally true. One might find it easier in theater to make the case that the producer is really the auteur, the central vision of the production, rather than anyone else. In film, we would almost always attach the 'auteur' label to the director.

Another unique aspect of theater is the intermission. While I do remember it as a norm in film when I was a youngster, it's virtually unheard of at the multiplex these days. Blessed with an intermission in theater, I usually make my way into the lobby, get a drink and generally observe the theater-goers. What are they saying? Occasionally I'll hear a funny line or an interesting insight. Are they leaving? Are people giving up on the play? What's the buzz? I'm certainly going to write what I feel, but intermission helps me take the pulse of the public. Later, when the curtain falls, how is the performance received? Is the audience enthusiastic? Are there curtain calls? These are things we really don't encounter in film. Although I must admit, when I took my kids to see *Herbie Reloaded* (2005) there was applause at the end. Herbie, however, never rolled out for a curtain call.

One of the most interesting differences between film and theater is the notion that 'the show must go on'. In film there is this wonderful, often used word, "Cut!" In theater, once the curtain rises, there's no such word. That adds a new dimension to the review. What were these actors faced with that might have hindered the live performance? I've seen sets collapse, malfunctioning special effects and actors forget lines. It's absolutely fascinating to see performers ad-lib to try and overcome the telephone that rings when it shouldn't and doesn't ring when it should. The biggest hurdle I ever witnessed took place at an outdoor, theater-in-the-round performance in Winnipeg, Canada. A local company was performing a summer Shakespeare piece when the clouds rolled in and the heavens literally poured. The greatest effects people have never produced a tempest like this. Actors running into the scene, slipped and slid across the stage, while the audience scrambled for cover (or their cars). Make-up streamed down faces. My wife and I stayed and watched in amazement as the performers continued on, drawing swords while thunder boomed all around. It was a moment totally unique to theater. The show did go on. And by the time the curtain fell (although there wasn't actually a curtain), the performance had outlasted the storm.

John Simon says in *Singularities*, "Love for the theater, certainly. But let us remember: *Qui bene amat, bene castigat* – who loves well, chastises well."(3) It's a wonderful point, but be clear that while 'chastising well' might call for tough love in the form of sharp criticism, it doesn't necessarily demand it. Were lines flubbed, entrances blown and other blemishes strewn upon the face of the play in wet Winnipeg? Absolutely, but one's 'love for the theater' would cause you to weigh them against the tropical storm that shared the stage. 'Chastising well', at least in my mind, demands accuracy and context in an effort to be fair, which is a tenet in the critic's quest for truth.

Chapter 5

Now Playing! *Ethical Concerns*

Starring.... The Critic

Co-Starring.... Influence

With a Special Appearance by... Dishonesty

Held Over for a 2nd Smash Week!

"*EC* is unforgettable!"

Frank Jones, *The Freebie Gazette*

"*EC* is the class of the summer season!"

Michelle Smith, *Daily Ego*

"Sure to be remembered at the Oscars!"

Kim Doe, *The Shady Dealer*

"Drama with a capital 'D'!!!"

Joe Bloe, *Weekly Sycophant*

If you think that critics don't face ethical issues, concerns or dilemmas, you're mistaken. Critics can be exposed to powerful influences and tempting desires. It's important to understand that in many cases, the ethical concerns faced by a critic at a large publication in a major or national market are not quite the same as the concerns faced by critics at mid level or smaller publications. At the very least, you're looking at different budgets, different circulations and different opportunities.

Larger publications have budgets that pay for more of the critic's expenses. A writer can be flown to Paris or Phoenix to see what's happening on the set of Tom Cruise's latest film. The magazine or newspaper absorbs the costs and owes the studio nothing, no favors either. The writer is free to praise the film lavishly or take it apart frame by frame. Just like some mega-stars are described as 'critic proof,' something similar might be said for the nation's largest magazines and newspapers. Because they provide so much coverage and have the potential to sell so many tickets, they're somewhat 'studio proof.' No matter how unflattering the resulting coverage might be; the studio is not likely to deny access to big players like a *Newsweek* or a *Los Angeles Times*.

At smaller publications, even national ones, the critic could be placed into a more precarious position. I've known publishers and editors who love when studios offer junkets to their writers. A junket, by the way, is when the studio provides an all expense paid trip to the set or location of a film with the hope that the critic will provide useful copy about the project. *The New York Times* reported in 1978 that a junket usually, "... lasts two days, costs (the studio) between $25,000 and $50,000, and consists of flying between 28 to 40 print and television journalists to Los Angeles for a screening, a relatively modest buffet dinner afterwards, and a day of interviews with the stars, director and producers." (1) But professor H. Eugene Goodwin of Penn State University adds, "... Universal Studios recently flew 50 journalists to Athens for five all-expense-paid days of boat trips to Greek islands, interviews with the stars, and a preview look at *The Greek Tycoon,* a movie that needed more than a junket to save it." (2) A colleague of mine was once flown to the Bahamas to sponge dive with a mid-level actress from her private yacht while she was filming a rather mediocre film. I was sitting in his office when they called and asked him if he thought there was a story or two in the junket. He envisioned several stories, then hung up the phone and called his travel agent on their dime while he set up his weekend retreat on a yacht in the Bahamas.

Well-known German director Wim Wenders believes behavior like this has contributed to the "decline of film criticism."

> "It's very hard to find critics or a magazine today that will
> publish material that is genuinely independent and written
> without any concern about being cut off some distributor's
> list or not be invited or flown into screenings. Many of the
> critics today get airline tickets, hotel accommodation, bags,
> beautiful photographs, gifts and other expenses paid by the
> distributors, and then are supposed to write serious articles
> about the movie. How can they write anything independent
> under these circumstances? They can't. Their living consists
> of working and writing for the distributors....
>
> The culture of independent film criticism has totally gone
> down the drain and this seems to come with the territory
> of the consumer age that we are now living in. Everything is
> entertainment; criticism is now entertainment..." (3)

Critics at smaller magazines and newspapers can feel pressure from their bosses to take advantage of these opportunities and cultivate them. A junket saves money, gets the writer good access and often provides celebrity stories that readers respond to. But the writer might also feel pressure from the studio to 'play nice.' If the filmmakers pay your way and you slam them too hard, it's possible that you won't be invited back. That might upset your editor or publisher who values free access. I've also seen writers who have so much fun on junkets that they can't wait to schedule another one. Many of them don't miss the opportunity to log some frequent flier miles on their personal accounts at the studio's expense. It can become a very slippery slope. That's one reason why *The Society of Professional Journalists, Sigma Delta Chi's* Code of Ethics states, "Journalists who use their professional status as representatives of the public for selfish or other unworthy motives violate a high trust.... Gifts, favors, free travel, special treatment or privileges can compromise the integrity of journalists and their employers. Nothing of value should be accepted."(4) While the term "value" is somewhat gray, the spirit of the ethic is certainly clear.

Another situation that gets the ethical radar beeping has to do with poster quotes, also known as, the blurb. Like the comments that appear at the start of this chapter, a complimentary line surgically sliced from a review can sell tickets. The most attractive lines for studios to quote are usually produced by well-known critics writing for powerhouse publications. Roger Ebert, who in 1975 was the first film critic in the nation to win a Pulitzer Prize for journalistic criticism, has faced this issue before. He writes, "I do not give blurbs to advertisers before my review has appeared. People will sometimes call up and say, 'Can we have a line for our ad?' and I don't do that. Once my review has appeared or once it has been written or broadcast or taped, then they are welcome to quote from it if they want to." (5)

Since critics will be rubbing elbows with filmmakers and publicity people on a fairly regular basis, they should try to maintain some professional distance, just as we would expect our White House reporters not to be too cozy with the president. It can be difficult to apply sharp criticism to 'friends.' Any influence that the general public is not likely to encounter, that might impede the honest application of critical thought, should usually be avoided. Obviously, access to filmmakers in the course of covering one's beat is a necessity. Socializing outside the course of coverage, however, is not. Film scholar Phillip Lopate says, "I think it's a good idea not to develop such good friendships with people in the industry, because you can be manipulated." (6)

Critics should also refrain from putting themselves under the employment of a studio. Accepting a 'freelance' assignment to help work on some publicity project is bad form. Submitting screenplays, evaluating scripts and other related tasks that one might stand to gain from are not only unacceptable on a personal level, these entanglements would probably violate ethical codes adopted by the publication and/or profession. Roger Ebert points out, "... even if Steven Spielberg were my best friend and he were calling me up daily, asking me if I'd seen any good manuscripts or screenplays, it would be unethical for me to submit them to him. I would then be placing myself in a position of reviewing a movie that I'd had a hand in or asking him for a favor when I have to maintain arm's length from him." (7)

Richard Schickel of TIME, says, "I don't know of any respected critic who will participate – paid or unpaid – in the marketing of contemporary movies." (8) In other words, what the critic is suggesting is that if you do engage in this activity you cannot be a 'respected' critic.

Kenneth Turin, well-known critic for the Los Angeles Times points out, "The people who read you should be confident there is absolutely nothing else on your mind. Accepting money from a studio has a potential to raise that question." (9)

Indeed, Fipresci, the International Federation of Film Critics founded in France in 1930, states in Article 6 - 4 of its statutes, "Registration [of any member] cannot be accepted if [there is]... a permanent or part time connection with production, distribution or advertising companies or institutions, or in films shot in recent years."

With the 'conglomerization' of media outlets; a merger frenzy that has made family owned newspapers the latest addition to the endangered species act, another ethical concern has arisen. In many, many cases, the paper employing the critic and the company that produced the film are subsidiaries of the same parent company. Could this develop into a conflict of interest?

Professor Mark Crispin Miller of New York University points out that within a week or so of the release of *Twister* (1996) by Warner Brothers Productions, TIME Magazine ran a cover story on hurricanes. The cover illustration looked remarkably like the movie poster. And, as you're probably guessing by now, both the magazine and the production company are subsidiaries of Time-Warner. Professor Miller says, "This phenomenon (mega media mergers) has had disastrous effects on what has been known as film criticism, film reviewing.... Now most film reviewers work for one or another of the same companies that make the movies.... You can't be a critic and a promoter at the same time. It's impossible." (10)

I have seen critics, often ones who might work at lesser-known or on-line publications, who will screen a film and know in the back of their minds that they've seen something that's instantly forgettable, that's really a failure. They also realize that the major critics at the big publications will likely not be providing quotable copy. A more corrupt critic might notice that the film has been produced by a large studio with a huge advertising budget. If they can find a few 'good' things to say, perhaps over-praise the effects or the acting, their comments might wind up on the poster or television commercials. And, as the film is promoted nationally, so are they. Ultimately, the public will forget the film, but they might remember the name of the critic and her publication; providing publicity for both, while garnering favor with the studio and filmmakers. It can be tempting. You're also promoting your paper or magazine, and some editors or publishers have no problem compromising cinematic/ethical standards to generate free publicity.

Allan Wolper reports in *Editor & Publisher*, a magazine that often serves as a newspaper industry watchdog, "The blurbs are so important that three years ago Sony executives created a fake movie critic, known as David Manning, to promote the studio's worst films." (11) Apparently the studio was releasing movies that were so bad, even corrupt critics wouldn't blurb them.

Wolper's article raises another important point when he writes that salespeople at *The New York Times* provide advance copies of the newspaper's reviews to studios to give them extra time to prepare promotional or, more importantly, advertising copy. The journalist speculates that this could also serve as an early warning that their movie might be panned. Wolper writes:

> "... *The New York Times* e-mails its movie reviews to
> studio publicists three hours before they are posted on
> the newspaper's Web site. The *Times* claims that its
> editorial integrity is not compromised because the reviews
> are already locked into the printing process, and can't be
> changed. But the message is clear: the alleged firewall
> between the newspaper's business and editorial sections
> has been breached." (12)

While one might think that a three-hour window is not very much, a lot can be accomplished during that time. Ads can be placed, pulled and campaigns can be re-worked. One is also forced to ask, where does this end? Who is entitled to this three-hour window? Is this opportunity only for high-spending Hollywood studios? Are politicians given this privilege? There is a saying in newspapers, "What we do for one, we do for all." Is this 'preview' a right that anyone can invoke, or is it merely available to deep-pocketed advertisers or those in positions of power? While *Times* executives might be able to explain away the policy, they could be damaged nonetheless by the appearance of an impropriety.

Under "Fairness" in *The Washington Post* Code of ethics, it says, "No story is fair if it consciously or unconsciously misleads or even deceives the reader. So fairness includes honesty – leveling with the reader." Critics should remember that they are journalists, in essence, writing stories. A review does not function as a 'get out of jail free card' with respect to ethical obligations.

On a more micro level, there are critics who seem to take personal satisfaction attacking performers and filmmakers in print. While *The New York Times Rule*, which basically states, "...'public figures' people who have 'thrust themselves' into public prominence, and even a few who have unwillingly been caught up in the vortex of newsworthy events – cannot recover libel damages in connection with reports of their public conduct unless they can show that whoever libeled them either knowingly lied or acted in reckless disregard of the truth, conduct that the Supreme Court called 'actual malice,' (13) would allow for such attacks from a legal standpoint, there are other considerations.

Critics should never lose sight of the fact that they are covering people. These directors, writers, actors, etc. should receive a basic level of respect, just as any human being would. So, is there no place for sarcasm or humor in a review? Mine are laced with both. I do hope that they are, however, presented professionally and fairly. While I have no intention of going soft on someone in a review, I also try not to be petty or unduly vicious. In his book *Sontag & Kael*, Craig Seligman writes:

> "Niceness, in criticism, is a form of bad faith. Nature *is* red
> in tooth and claw, and distinguishing those who can from
> those who can't is the very first thing a critic has to do....
> 'Tactful' pans are no less damaging to artists' feelings than
> candid ones are, and the reader can sense their dishonesty.

Crude, flat pans are something else again. It can be sickening
to watch second-rate critics wielding their blunt instruments;
there is, as Dryden famously noted, 'a vast difference betwixt
the slovenly butchering of a man, and the fineness of a stroke
that separates the head from the body, and leaves it standing
in its place.'" (14)

Responding to a charge of excessively harsh criticism from British playwriter/
director David Hare, *New York Times* theater critic Frank Rich provides a different
perspective on 'niceness in criticism' by saying:

"... [If Mr. Hare believes that] I have an obligation to protect
serious theater by softening my criticism so that people might
go see it to preserve serious theater rather than because it's a
good evening of theater, I completely disagree with him. I
think that if I were to shilly-shally and send people to serious
theater that in my heart I knew was kind of dull, I would be
doing the theater a disservice, because those people are not
going to come back again." (15)

It would seem that Rich has decided that his obligation to write honestly about
what he sees on stage, combined with his priority to serve his readers before he serves
the theater, prevents him from endorsing productions that arguably might add to the
health of the arts, while boring the audience at their expense. I personally find it
interesting that Mr. Hare does not hesitate to point out the critic's alleged mandate to
'support the arts', yet apparently ignores the critic's obligations to speak truth to his

readers and to function as a journalist employed by a newspaper. If the film critics are obligated to 'support the arts' by tempering their criticism, then one could argue that a sportswriter is obligated to support the team (or the sport), or the political writer is obligated to support the administration or the current initiative. Most thinking people would not want journalists who are 'supporters'. That would undermine the First Amendment and the basic function of a free press. Criticism should not be a function of Public Relations. Given the choice between honesty and cheerleading from critics, I'll take honesty every time.

Critics not only write *about* people, they write *to* people. Some critics make a habit of attacking, albeit insulting, readers who might not share their taste. That's something I try never to do. Anyone who purchases your publication and then takes the time to give you their attention deserves a certain level of critical decorum. You should be able to make your points without stooping to *ad hominem* leveled at the reader. Renata Adler, former chief film critic at the *New York Times*, took issue with critics who humiliate readers when she told a Boston University audience, "It (your review) cannot be an attack to the audience that might like the thing. It just doesn't seem fair." (16)

There are those people (editors among them) who would maintain that while the critic should express her opinion about the elements of the film, the critic should refrain from sharing her own views on the issues covered by the film. The review is, after all, about the movie, not the critic.

Yes, there is some truth to this, but it's not an all or nothing case. If a critic who feels strongly about the war in Iraq and/or George Bush is reviewing *Fahrenheit 9/11*, those views can color the way in which the critic interprets what's on screen. So, what we're really talking about is a question of balance. How much personal disclosure should the critic share? When is one's opinion about a film actually an opinion about something else? Does it matter? Does it help? Does it get in the way?

I wish I had a simple, one-size-fits-all answer to this, but these are complex questions that are better addressed on a case-by-case basis. What's really important here is that the critic is in touch with personal opinions and wields them carefully, selectively and with restraint.

Owen Gleiberman, a critic at *Entertainment Weekly*, recently wrote:

> "...why, in reviewing *An Inconvenient Truth*, did I state
> unequivocally that I agree with Al Gore's views on global
> warming? Several readers objected – not just to my opinion,
> but to the fact that I'd deign to include that opinion in a
> review. *Stick to the movie*, they said. Yet is it desirable,
> or even possible?
>
> When you write about a documentary, you're evaluating,
> among other things, how well it penetrates and defines
> a particular subject, be it Rudy Giuliani, the war in Iraq,
> or the Pop art scene of the 1960s. To omit your own thoughts
> and feelings wouldn't just be dishonest, it would be fruitless
> and boring – the reduction of reality to a vacuum.
>
> That said, there's a difference between writing that reflects
> a critic's politics and writing that's ruled by them. I've seen
> [documentaries] I agreed with politically yet questioned as
> films, like *Fahrenheit 9/11* or *The Corporation*. The goal is
> to be open minded, which requires revealing one's mind." (17)

Even though Gleiberman is speaking more directly about documentaries here, I would argue that much of what he points out, certainly the spirit of it, is also pertinent when one covers feature films. We are human beings, brimming with opinions and biases. Whether we state them or not, they exist. As critics, we are also communicators, journalists. For readers to understand the perspectives of our professional opinions, it can be vital that the critic share personal opinions that are related to the film. One of the tricky parts, beyond the question of over indulgence, is that we recognize that our opinions might not be valid for other viewers. Where we see problems, others might find perfection, and vice versa. So, while it's imperative that the critic open his mind and share it with readers, it's just as vital that the same critic maintain an open mind. You will have greater perspective. You will see more. You will be more interesting and knowledgeable when your mind serves as fertile ground for images and ideas that challenge your beliefs. This is not to say that the critic accept everything she/he sees. Critics merely need to give films fair consideration. And then, let the chips fall where they may.

Chapter 6

Thoughts on how to get a job.

"Will write for popcorn."

Obviously, there's no foolproof, easy-to-follow method to get a job as a film critic. Let's face it, it's a job that many people would like to have, and yet, there are a limited number of opportunities out there. However, when I was an undergraduate at Clark University deciding what I wanted to do with my life, I didn't allow those two considerations to deter me. I figured that someone was going to get hired to be a critic, why not me? Ah, but that begged the question; "Why would anyone hire *me*?" The simple answer is, because you know so much about movies, communicate your thoughts with so much style and insight that readers will be engaged on a regular basis. This is what an editor would be willing to pay for. But how does one get there from here, I wondered.

As a freshman in college, having successfully completed my first film class, Prof. Anthony Hodgekinson's Introduction to Film, I knew I had fallen in love with 'the cinema'. I also knew that no editor in her right mind would *pay* me to write reviews, nor would readers find them worth their time, so I set out to remedy the situation. Immediately, I declared a double major in English and Screen Studies and joined The Scarlet (the school newspaper) as its film critic. I went to classes, read other critics regularly, attended every on-campus screening, joined the university film society and began my journey.

William L. Rivers offers sage advice for the fledgling critic in his text, *Writing Opinion: Reviews*. He says, "Judgements of works of art are so diverse and critics come from such varying backgrounds that there is no precise standard in any field. Nor can there be one. The most that can be said is that becoming a critic requires years of study – and familiarity with the work of the best critics in one's field."(1) One of the key words here is 'familiarity'. It's a good word, not overstated at all. Years of study, yes. But that does not mean that you must be a living, breathing cinematic encyclopedia. There are encyclopedias for that. You need to know your film, make no mistake, but just because you'd do well on *Jeopardy* or playing Trivial Pursuit, does not mean you have insight into what's happening on screen. That's a higher calling built on a foundation of solid film knowledge.

When asked, "What is your basis for judging a movie?" Pauline Kael replies:

> When one answers that new films are judged in terms of how
> they extend our experience and give us pleasure, and that our
> ways of judging how they do this are drawn not only from
> older films but from other works of art, and theories of art,
> that new films are generally related to what is going on in the
> other arts, that as wide a background as possible in literature,
> painting, music, philosophy, political thought, etc., helps, that
> it is the wealth and variety of what he has to bring to new works
> that makes the critic's reaction to them valuable, the questioners
> are always unsatisfied. They wanted a simple answer, a formula...
>
> And it is very difficult to such people that criticism is
> exciting just because there is no formula to apply, just because
> you must use everything you are and everything you know that
> is relevant, and that film criticism is particularly exciting just
> because of the multiplicity of elements in film art. (2)

By the time I graduated I had studied those 'best critics in one's field' that Professor Rivers speaks of, tried to widen my background as much as possible as Kael suggests, reviewed a pile of films, covered theater, television and music; interviewed several celebrities, wrote entertainment features and drove to New York City (at my own expense in a beat-up 1974 Ford Maverick) to attend several screenings (*Heaven's Gate* and *Napoleon* among them). I had also gained experience doing layout & design, assigning & editing stories and served as the paper's entertainment editor for two years. That's how my journey began. Yours doesn't have to mimic mine, but whatever path you choose, you will have to know your film and be able to write about it.

When you're looking for work, the first question any editor will ask is, "Do you have clips?" If all you can do is resurrect your Intro to Journalism midterm exam, it will also be the last question the editor asks and you'll be laughed out of the building. You need to be able to answer the query by sending in several gems with your resume and/or laying down an impressive portfolio of your published work (student publications count) on the editor's desk. There's no substitute for this. The clips (ie: your published writing) will speak for themselves. No editor ever asked me how I did on my *History of American Journalism* oral report, but every editor who ever interviewed me (and there were many) asked to see my clips. Doing well in your classes is a wonderful achievement, but you need to do more than that... write!

Legendary film critic Andrew Sarris of *Village Voice* fame, wrote in *Confessions of a Cultist* that having joined *Film Culture* as a reviewer/editor in 1955, "I was not enchanted by the prospect of writing and editing for no money at all. It seemed almost as demeaning as paying to be published, an act of vanity I vowed never to perform even at the cost of immortality. However, my bargaining position was not enhanced by the fact that all my previous professional writing credits added up to seven movie columns in the

Fort Devens *Dispatch*…"(3) Sarris, nonetheless, accepted the position and is now widely recognized as a heavyweight in the history of film criticism. It's the good thing he had those clips.

Roger Ebert began college as an English major. After his second year, he became a journalism major. Ebert wrote for the student paper, the *Daily Illini*, and by his senior year he was the editor. "I never took a single class on film or film criticism," he remembers. "There weren't any film classes at the University of Illinois when I was there. I went to a lot of films – the campus film society, the cinema international. I had written reviews for the *Daily Illini*. But I didn't have it on my agenda that I was going to be a critic until they gave me the job. I had written about movies for the *Sun-Times*, and the previous film critic retired." (4)

No one wants to pay a critic to hold his hand and teach him. Editors usually hire writers who are seasoned, self-motivated and professional. Ahhh, but now you protest, that's a Catch-22 (a great book/film by the way)! If I need to be seasoned to get seasoned, how will that ever happen? It's really a matter of levels. The amount of experience needed to write for the student newspaper is substantially less than the amount of experience needed to review for TIME. By doing the former, one will get closer to doing the latter. Start at your student publication and take the right classes. But even that's not cast in stone. *The New York Times*' Janet Maslin was a math major in college. (5) If you're not in school, educate yourself. Read the right books, read other critics regularly and see tons of films. Don't just go to the video store. Go to the library and occasionally screen films that the masses aren't necessarily seeing. Not only is the library's collection usually more eclectic than the local video store's, movies that are borrowed and returned on time are free. If you can afford it, try a basic on-line membership to a movie service, a la Netflix or Blockbuster.

If you want work, you'll still need current clips. Try to find a local paper, maybe a free weekly or monthly where they'll let you cover films. A decent on-line publication might also do the trick if your reviews are well done. Film Scholar Phillip Lopate sees online opportunities as a viable path for novice critics.

"I'm excited that people who wouldn't have many venues to break into will have a chance to learn a craft and to experiment. It's proof that there's a great need to write about movies – not only is film criticism not dead, but you've got a lot of amateurs out there who are trying to do it and some of them will become film critics. So I don't feel at all threatened by that, I think it's great. When young wannabe critics turn to me and ask where they can get published, there aren't that many places, so the web is a salvation in a way.

But of course you need to get paid, that's the problem! But you can hone your craft, you can learn a lot – how to approach a movie, quickly get a take on it and how to approach a piece. You have to start somewhere. As a writer I began at open mic Poetry readings. Everybody has to start somewhere." (6)

Even if you don't get paid at first, having good current clips can be better than money in the bank when you're competing for a position. Use your association with the smaller publication to showcase your abilities and to pave the way to bigger things. Network with studio publicity people to get access to celebrities, to book interviews, attend press conferences and screenings. Take time to connect with other critics and editors.

Without being a nuisance, and understanding that you will be ignored by the vast majority of those who you approach, send a clip now and then to other editors and writers who might be able to mentor or guide you. Always thank anyone who takes any interest in your career. At this stage of your development, and considering that you're asking them to help you, *their* time is more valuable than *yours*.

 Be patient. Advancement, opportunity and growth take time. And all these take the most time when you're just starting out. The further along you get, the easier things become, as you build upon past successes. It certainly helps to be lucky, but to a large degree you make your own luck. Those who are more prepared, more skilled, more motivated, more experienced; tend to get 'luckier' than those who are not.

 There are websites and publications that can give you listings of opportunities, although 'Film Critic' isn't exactly a heading in the *New York Times* Classified section. (I'd check it anyway.) Look under *reporter, editor, writer, publishing, magazines, newspapers, journalist,* and whatever else you can think of. Be creative in your search. Academics, librarians and journalists can be helpful here. I've always had good luck with *Editor & Publisher Magazine* and the *Sunday New York Times.*

 'You *can* get there from here.' Again, Janet Maslin is proof. She was covering film for the *Boston Phoenix,* a weekly not unlike New York's *Village Voice,* when the *New York Times* hired her. (7) While one might not expect the *Times* to hire its film critics from smaller weeklies, it just goes to show that there's nothing like being good at what you do. Once the review is printed, whatever the publication, the talent (or lack of) has been displayed and it becomes a matter of record. The proof, as they say, is in the pudding, so keep making pudding if you really want the job.

 Even when you're writing about film, try to expand what you do. Don't pigeon-hole yourself. If you're primarily a critic, make sure you also write related film stories (interviews, previews, issue pieces, etc.) that take you beyond the standard review. With that in mind, you will be much more marketable if you can do other things beyond movies. Can you cover theater? How about television, art, music? The more times you can say 'yes' to an editor, the more likely you are to get hired. But in this business, just saying yes isn't enough. You will have to have clips to back up the claim. Be prepared to add interviews, previews, CD reviews, theater reviews and other entertainment pieces to your portfolio.

If the idea that expanding your entertainment background can make it more likely to get opportunity as a critic makes sense to you, then let's take it a step further. Many publications, especially those hiring entry level reporters, won't have a full-time spot for a film critic, or maybe even an entertainment reporter. Again, you will find yourself in a more marketable position if you can provide evidence (ie: clips) that show you have done general assignment reporting (school boards, local government and the like), some sports, an op-ed or two, and of course, news. Those types of experiences will allow you to be hired as a general assignment reporter who can sneak over to the entertainment desk whenever you're needed. Once you prove yourself, a more permanent entertainment position might follow. At the very least, you'll be able to gather more ammunition (ie: clips) for the next entertainment opening you pursue. If you do wind up on the entertainment desk, continue with the same strategy, covering anything you're sent to, but always volunteering to write film. When the film critic is away on vacation, without being too pushy, volunteer to screen movies in her absence.

Remember, the people who don't do the basic things, who aren't willing to pay their dues won't get or keep the jobs. I went to college with several writers who were much more talented than me. A few months after graduation, I accepted a job as a bodyguard at CBS for $10,000 a year. I saw it as foot-in-the-door. I would keep looking for something better, but I might get lucky at the network. A classmate told me that he would never work for $10,000 a year. Well, he was half right. He would never work, not as a journalist. No one was going to come out of the blue and lay a $40,000 a year position on him straight out of college. While it was difficult back then commuting to Manhattan on that salary, today I have a career as a journalist. My friend has a job. Try to take the long view, be patient and work hard. That CBS position helped me get to *Modern Screen*, which helped me get to *ROCKbeat*, which helped me get to *Inside Books*, which helped me get to Penn State, and then to Monmouth University, and later, to get novels and even a textbook published. Many other critics will tell you similar stories about their careers. Had she not written for at the Boston *Phoenix*, Janet Maslin would not have been hired by *The New York Times*. Had he not accepted a position without pay at *Film Culture* or written reviews for the Fort Devens *Dispatch*, Andrew Sarris wouldn't have made a name for himself at New York's *Village Voice*. Had he not attended screenings from college film societies and written reviews for the *Daily Illini*, Roger Ebert would likely not have wound up at as the Pulitzer prize winning critic at the *Sun Times*. A career is a journey that must be made one step at a time, but only you can take those steps. Hopefully this text will help you along your way.

Sample Reviews

Learn from my mistakes.

The following reviews are my own. After each review, I've included comments identifying the techniques I employed. While reviews from critics like Maslin, Kael, Ebert, Agee, Corliss and many others would likely provide much more compelling copy, I'm unable to tell you how their reviews were written or what was going on in the writer's mind when the lines were composed. By using my own work, I'm able to comment on intent and process from a closer perspective. The main goal is to give readers some insight, a little background between the lines, if you will, with regard to how these pieces were written. You should be able to see many of the elements discussed in the text put to use. Perhaps seeing them featured in an actual review will help you apply the concepts to your work in your own unique way.

Fahrenheit 9/11

IS IT THE TRUTH, OR IS IT MOORE?

by John Morano

Is Michael Moore's controversial *Fahrenheit 911* a documentary, a satire, an op-ed, propaganda, the truth, a lie, disrespectful, an expose', an act of patriotism, an act of capitalism? Yes, it is.

That's the easy answer. The harder part is to decide where to place each of those labels within the framework of the film. For me, as a critic and a professor of journalism, I would call Moore's movie a 'prop-ed', two parts propaganda, one part opinion/editorial. But keep in mind, just because something is labeled propaganda, or op-ed for that matter, that doesn't mean the content is necessarily untrue. There is certainly plenty of truth in Moore's film. As a journalist, however, I'm forced to ask, 'What truths?' and 'Whose are they?' To answer the latter; in part, they're certainly Moore's.

At a crisp 91 minutes, *Fahrenheit 911* is a blanket indictment against President Bush and all the president's 'men', as it were. Moore goes straight for the jugular as he depicts conspiracy theories that make the second gunman theory of the Kennedy assassination look like basic arithmetic. Much of what Moore presents is compelling and thought provoking. Other moments are simplistic, anecdotal and unfair. In a way, he's the anti-Rush Lembaugh... he's Leftbaugh.

The film is painstakingly pieced together with world class editing and very sophisticated use of music to enhance the comments being made. Moore has a great eye for irony and is a master of juxtaposition. For example, in a scene where *uniformed* secret service agents (an oxymoron if ever I saw one) question Moore about his filming outside the Saudi Embassy, Moore inquires, "Do you normally give security to foreign embassies?" When the

The Presidency of George Bush is the focal point of the latest entry by Michael Moore.

Fahrenheit 9/11
(Lion's Gate)
Starring: Michael Moore
"PG-13"
For Violent and Disturbing Images, Language
★★★★

officer replies that he doesn't, Moore follows up with, "So, do the Saudis give you more trouble than other embassies?" This time the officer says, "I'm not allowed to comment on questions like that." Moore smiles and concludes, "I'll take that as a yes." And that's the director's biggest problem. He's his own worst enemy because he's too ready to assign his own biased answer to the question. The man said he wasn't allowed to comment. He didn't say yes, or no. As a result, Moore chips away at his own credibility and makes it easier for those who want to dismiss his other more poignant and telling criticisms.

When Moore discusses Bush's missed medical exam while the president was a reservist during the Vietnam war, the director plays a few bars of Eric Clapton's hit *Cocaine*. The implication is obvious (Bush would not have passed his blood test), but while making this charge in a comic, unsubstantiated fashion makes for good theater, ethically and credibly it's weak, making it easy for those who'd like to, to reject the charge... and by extension, others.

Fahrenheit 911 is more polished than Moore's previous *Roger & Me* and academy award winning *Bowling for Columbine,* but it's also more over the top. In its own way, the film is as passionate a picture as Mel Gibson's *The Passion of Christ.* Both directors were criticized for

allowing their personal beliefs to dictate what ultimately appeared on screen. And both directors received massive publicity and box office as a result. But that's pretty much where the comparisons end.

For me, some of the most memorable, most powerful moments came, not when Moore provided his omniscient, sarcastic narration, but when he allowed average Americans to speak for themselves; the Flint, Michigan mother who lost her son to the war; the soldiers on duty in Iraq talking about what cd's they played in the tank during battle; and the two elderly women sitting in a bingo parlor chatting about the day's news, making more sense than any of the politicians or corporate elite. For Moore, one step backward is often two steps forward.

I was personally pleased that when he examined the events of September 11th Moore refrained from showing the towers being struck by the planes. Instead, he relied on reaction shots of people on the street. However, when he discussed the war in Iraq, there were no shortage of graphic clips of injured civilians. It was a very disturbing sequence, but helped bring home the point that war is not an abstraction. It is real for everyone involved. Everyone suffers. And that's where the film is at its best.

At times the movie reminded me of a film version of Joe

McGinniss's book *The Selling of the President 1968.* Some of the things Moore does to Bush reek of what McGinniss did to Nixon. Both, for instance, have little trouble telling viewers/ readers what people are 'thinking'. Again, as a journalist, I've never been quite able to master that one. Those of you familiar with Noam Chomsky will probably see some parallels as well, especially with respect to mass fear and the herd mentality. I also wondered why Moore was able to get footage from military personnel that the mainstream press seemed to have so collectively missed. Perhaps the press is still reeling from the Vietnam effect (a war lost because of press coverage), which the media claim isn't their fault (Don't shoot the messenger...). I left the theater wondering, "Do we really have to rely on Michael Moore to keep us fully informed?"

Fahrenheit 911 is neither the 'whole truth' nor 'nothing but the truth'... but there are moments of truth, unpleasant truths, and truths that some would rather you didn't hear; which gives the film value.

My question for Moore is, now that you've broken box-office records for documentary dollars, what are you going to do with your millions? Will you help your people in Flint, Michigan whom you tell us about regularly? Will you donate to victims of 9/11? Will you help provide some limited relief for those poor civilians in Iraq? Perhaps you're already doing those things. One would hope so, because otherwise, on one level, you'd be just as bad as the Haliburtons of the world, profiting from the pain of others. And one day, someone would be forced to make an expose' film called *Michael & Me.*

The bottom line here is, if you walk into the theater hating Michael Moore, you'll probably walk out hating him. If you walk into the theater loving Michael Moore, you'll probably walk out loving him. If you're somewhere in between, try to approach the film with a critically opened mind. In other words, be skeptical, but be open. And don't let some biased pundit tell you what it all means. Don't even let Moore do that. For me, this is one of those rare moments when a film deserves to be called 'important'.

Fahrenheit 9/11

(2004)

Col. 1, paragraph 1:

Since so many people were so divided about what the film actually was, I thought I'd lead with a Q & A that pretty much covered the range of reactions that the film would generate among various viewers.

Col. 1, paragraph 2:

Line 5: I'm giving a quick disclosure so that readers can judge what perspective I'm coming from.

Line 7: I love to play with the language, so I've created my own word "prop-ed". I'm trying to have a little fun and stimulate thought at the same time.

Col. 1, paragraph 3:

Line 1: I slip an adjective in front of the running time so that I can accomplish more than just present the time. I can, with one 'crisp' word, also give the readers a sense of whether the film dragged or not. Try to multi-task with your writing.

Line 7: Since we are looking at a film that deals with history and conspiracy theories, it seemed logical to draw on the Kennedy assassination as an example. Allow the subject of the film to influence the language and images that you choose.

Line 16 (last line): Sometimes I just can't stop myself. 'Leftbaugh' was too much fun to leave on the cutting room floor. And, as long as you don't overindulge, it's okay to be *you*.

Col. 1, paragraph 4:

Line 1: 'painstakingly pieced'... Like a good spice when cooking, a *little* alliteration can add flavor, but too much can be difficult to digest.

Line 6: Assonance also works... And as long as I'm making a claim about irony, I should also include an example of what I mean from the text, hence the next several lines.

Col. 2, top graph:

Line 10: Once you make a comment and then provide an example, don't always assume that readers will come to the same conclusion you have. Follow the example up with some brief interpretation. Lead them comfortably through your thought and you're less likely to be misunderstood.

Col. 2, paragraph 2:

Line 6: Again, don't assume the readers will understand your point. Lay it neatly out there for them, hence the parenthetical comment.

Col. 2, last graph:

Both *The Passion* and *Fahrenheit 911* were contemporaries, and blockbusters. If you see similarities between them, discuss them. It's timely and will likely speak to your target audience.

Col. 3, first full graph:

If you're going to tell readers where the film fails, in the interests of balance and completeness, you should also point out where it succeeds.

Last graph: If you're going to speak about other films and/or historical events that pertain to *Fahrenheit 911*, when appropriate, there's no reason to stop there. Why not mention literature, theater, music, art, thinkers, etc. that might enliven the review?

Col. 4, paragraph 3:

When a film, via its director, writer, performers, etc. comments on an issue or tells us what we should or shouldn't do; don't be afraid to hold those espousing the action to the ethic themselves. Do they practice what they preach? And in this case, it seemed fair to turn the table on Mr. Moore for a moment.

Last paragraph:

Present some summary thought, hopefully a useful one, and try to end with a little pizzazz.

SCREEN

No Need to Dodge Dodgeball

DODGEBALL IS A GOOD COMIC FILM

by John Morano

"LINE TO LINE!"... The words echo in my mind as if I heard them this morning. Actually, the last time I heard that phrase, it was spoken by my 6th grade gym teacher, who screamed it out with maniacal satisfaction... About halfway through a typical gym class dodgeball game, he'd scream the dreaded "Line to Line" and then, instead of being thrown at from half-court, players were allowed to wind up from the closest foul-line. And even though it's been, dare I say, 30 years, I can still feel the sting of the small, over-inflated rubber balls.

In *Dodgeball: A True Underdog Story*, when a young Patches O'Houlihan (Hank Azaria), perennial AADA all-star, tells school children in a training film, "Dodgeball is a sport of violence, exclusion and degradation." it becomes obvious that the filmmakers feel our pain. They too remember the taste of rubber against a bloodied lip.

As traumatizing as the game of dodgeball might have been for some, the film is a much friendlier feature. Written and directed by Rawson Marshall Thurber, starring Ben Stiller as White Goodman and Vince Vaughn as Peter La Fleur, the film follows in the footsteps of National Lampoon and *Saturday Night Live* wackiness. It's a weird satirical comedy that has

Ben Stiller in Dodgeball.

Dodgeball: A True Underdog Story
(20th Century Fox)
**Starring: Ben Stiller,
Vince Vaughan, Christine Taylor**
"PG-13"
For Rude, Sexual Humor, & Language
★★★☆

charm and laughs.

White Goodman owns Globo Gym, whose motto is, "We're better than you and we know it." He decides to buy-out the mortgage of his rival across the street, Average Joe's Gym, owned by the average Peter La Fleur. La Fleur and his collection of misfits have 30 days to raise $50,000 or they lose their gym to Goodman. There are several sub-plots that are definitely sub-par. The film is as predictable as a pull-up, but still manages to entertain.

Stiller is wonderful as the owner of Globo Gym who guarantees to turn anyone who "hates themselves enough" from a "Frankenstein into a Frankenfine". Vaugn's La Fleur, on the other hand, has a good day if his ancient, rusted-out Pontiac starts in the morning. The actors have a nice on-screen chemistry and genuinely seem to have had a blast making this film. I can't imagine how many scenes needed to be re-shot because cast members were laughing at each other.

Two supporting players worth mentioning are Stephen Root and Christine Taylor. Root, who

many will remember for his role as Jimmy James in television's *NewsRadio* (1995-99) gives audiences a chuckle as Gordon. Taylor, who seems like the reincarnation of Marsha Brady (she actually played her in *A Very Brady Sequel*) does a good job with what Thurber has given her.

Really, what makes the film shine are the scenes that involve dodgeball, with one of the best being the qualifying round when the Average Joes play a troop of girl scouts. Matches at the national tournament in Las Vegas, which appear on ESPN 8 'The Ocho,' are a little too rushed. As the film progresses, it evolves(?) into a mix of *Slapshot* and *The Karate Kid*... maybe with a touch of *Caddyshack* woven into its fabric. And as long as we're talking *Caddyshack*, the referee in the dodgeball tournament, Al Kaplon (who does a fair job) would have been so much more interesting had Bill Murray been cast. *Dodgeball* is chock full of cameos. Look for David Hasselhoff, Lance Armstrong, Chuck Norris and William Shatner, among others.

The satirical comedy is not without deep messages. La Fleur tells us that if you live life without goals, you can never be disappointed. I guess when you get pelted in the head enough times with dodgeballs, you're able to uncover philosophical truths. (Had Bertrand Russell only known.) The elder Patches O'Houlihan, played with gusto by Rip Torn, tells us, "If you can dodge a wrench, you can dodge a ball." (I wish someone had told me that in 6th grade.) And personally, the movie taught me that no matter how many times you see someone get hit in the groin with a blazing dodgeball, it never ceases to be funny.

If you appreciate better production values, an inspired camera, graceful editing, etc., *Dodgeball* is strictly 'average Joe'. The soundtrack, however, is surprisingly lively and Carol Ramsey's costumes are pretty good.

The film is appropriately rated PG-13 for "rude and sexual humor, and language". I wouldn't bring *my* kids to this one. They can rent it with their pals on a Friday night when they get a little older. At roughly 100 minutes, *Dodgeball* bounces along at a good pace, not dragging at all. While it's a good date film, there's no need to see it on the big screen and drop $8.75 a ticket. It will be a great rental in a few months, perfect for the DVD player and the couch.

Early in the film, a skeptical Peter La Fleur says, "There's no way we're gonna get $50,000 for playing dodgeball." In one sense he's right. If the opening weekend box office is any indication, they're gonna get more like $100,000,000 for playing dodgeball. It may not be *Tootsie* or *Citizen Kane*, but for folks who are still in touch with their inner child and appreciate the Zen of *Caddyshack*'s, "Be the ball," *Dodgeball* will be a fun game.

114

Dodgeball
(2004)

Col. 1, paragraph 1:

When you go see a film like *Dodgeball*, most of us have a pretty good idea what we're getting into. In the spirit of the film, as a critic you might relax a bit on the page and raise the level of humor and lower (just a touch, mind you) the level of deep reflective criticism. With that in mind, the lead harkens back to when *I* played the game as a youngster. Hopefully, it serves as a good vehicle to launch the review.

Col. 1, paragraph 2:

Line 6: I loved the quote when I heard it on screen, so I wrote it down in my notes. Often, if it makes you smile, many readers will too. I still grin every time I read or hear that quote.

Col. 1, paragraph 3:

Line 3: 'film, friendly, feature'... a pinch of alliteration.

Col 2, paragraph 1:

I've waited about as long as you really can to get to the plot summary. Try to do it quickly and completely (it can be a tough balance) without giving too much away.

Line 12: As referred to earlier in the text, this is where I changed "as predictable as a sunrise" to "as predictable as a pull-up."

Col. 2, last paragraph:

It's usually a good idea to mention supporting players who were, for whatever reason, especially memorable.

Col. 4, first paragraph:

Even in an oddball comedy, themes and messages can be identified. In this case, the film was so wacky I tried to reflect that in my comments.

Col. 4, paragraph 2:

First sentence: Use the language of the film 'average Joe' to make your comment.

Col. 4, last paragraph:

Again, round out the review, sum up your general feeling and try to end with a little literary bling.

STAR WARS EPISODE 3

Warp speed action

by John Morano

When Darth Sidious commands General Grievous to perpetrate one of his foul plots, the droid replies, "It will be done, my lord." But when George Lucas commands his army of viewers to pony up $9 and 2 hours and 41 minutes of their time, will they reply likewise?... Apparently so, if the initial $50 million weekend for *Star Wars: Episode III - Revenge of the Sith* is any indication. While this third episode is the final installment (so claims Lucas) of the Star Wars film saga, it's pretty clear that this series will end with a BANG and not a whimper, both fiscally and dramatically.

The plot, for those of you who have been living on an asteroid in the Naboo Quadrant, revolves around Anakin Skywalker's descent into the Dark Side. The Clone Wars have dragged on for three years. The Jedi Council and the Senate are at odds. And Anakin is caught in the middle. Will he follow the teachings of Obi-Wan and Yoda, or will he side with Supreme Chancellor Palpatine? Take a wild guess...

Right from the start, the jaw-dropping, IMAXian space battle reminds us of one reason why Lucas has been so successful. This is a spectacle built on Oscar worthy special effects from the visionaries at Industrial Light and Magic. Huge Battle Cruisers fire broadside volleys like ancient schooners that once flew the Jolly-Roger. Explosions pepper the screen, while smaller fighters race by, dodging missiles (and critical thought). The swashbuckling scenario continues throughout the film (I counted no less than 15 separate light saber battles). Even Yoda manages an impressive Kermit-meets-Errol Flynn homage, in his own little green way.

And, as long as we're talking about *green* and Yoda, it's not hard to imagine the Jedi master quipping, "Twisted by the *Green* side, Master Lucas has become." For surely, if Star Wars is about anything, it's about money. Forget moments of familiar product placement where we might see Vader sipping a Coke or

Annakin Skywalker succombs to the dark side of the force in *Star Wars: Episode III*.

Obi driving an Audi. *Episode III* takes promotion to a new galaxy, but this one's no longer 'far far away'. In this movie, the entire film is product placement. *Everything* is for sale. I have two boys, ages 11 and 9. I can show you the credit card receipts. There's nothing on that screen that can't be purchased somewhere. So, in that sense, what we have here is the birth of the *filmercial*.

But let's talk about the *movie*. There are several good performances. Ewan McGregor, while not Oscar caliber, is wonderful as Obi-Wan; a fitting forebearer to the later incarnation by Sir Alec Guinness. Samuel Jackson as Mace Windu, leader of the Jedi Council, does a great job, making me lament that he did not have more screen time. Ian McDiarmid as Supreme Chancellor Palpatine is deliciously dark in his portrayal.

Hayden Christensen as Anakin is passable, but as such is disappointing. I had hoped for more. But even more disappointing is Natalie Portman as Padme (on whom I liked in *Closer*). Her stiff, monotoned, uninspired, lifeless depiction of the futuristic femme fatale stands, or should I say falls, in contrast to the pageant that Lucas produces all around her. When Padme and Anakin share the screen, the film

grinds to an almost unbearable halt as it descends into the dark depths of melodrama, while viewers twitch and shuffle waiting for the next light saber battle or reckless chase to ensue.

Beyond the more traditional actors; Grevous is great and it's wonderful to see R2-D2, C-3PO and Chewey return to the saga. There is, however, one actor worthy of Oscar consideration. Yoda deserves the statue for best performance by an alien playing an alien. Not since E.T. have I seen such a performance. And rumor has it, he did all his own stunts.

Other Oscar considerations should be given to the very tight editing, the inspired sound and the almost never-ending orchestrations; which brought to mind a variety of 1940's film classics. The costumes, the camera and again, the unparalleled special effects are all Oscar worthy. *Revenge of the Sith* features too many eye-popping scenes and special effects to list individually. Lucas gives new meaning to the 'conference call' with the Jedi Council meetings and the Dante-infernoesque final scenes are remarkable.

There are two curious moments that evoke images of Frances Ford Coppola. In one, a shadowed Yoda advises the distraught Anakin. The set-up of the scene is remarkably similar to those where Brando and Sheen discussed philosophy in *Apocalypse Now*. In another sequence, there is a musical montage of Jedi slayings that appears to be spawned by *The Godfather* executions. Throughout *Revenge of the Sith*, there are glimpses of films and cinematic influences that have moved Lucas.

When I think about the *Star Wars Saga* and look for some comparable standard to hold it to, I come up with *Lord of the Rings* and *Harry Potter*. From a production value and budget standpoint, *Star Wars*, to say the least, holds its own. But where it slips is with respect to the writing. In *Lord of the Rings*, you're hearing Tolkien. In *Harry Potter*, you're hearing Rowling. But with *Star Wars*, you're hearing Lucas. That hurts the films a bit. Lucas is a superb director/producer, but the writing is not nearly at the same level. Wookies attack battle droids and 'bots with laser *crossbows*? Jedi wear Bat-belts that have mini grappling hooks, underwater breathing devices and, of course, the ubiquitous light sabers. And, one character goes from not even

being a Jedi Master to Sith Lord in an instant. Just add water and... poof... you're a Sith Lord. I studied harder to get a driver's license.

That being said, Lucas did surprise me with one of his main themes in *Revenge of the Sith*. I'll list several quotes from the film. You tell me what's on George's mind.

Anakin - "I think this war is destroying the principles of the Republic."

Padme - "This war represents a failure [of government] to listen."

Padme - "What if this was not the democracy we believed in?"

Chancellor Palpatine - "Good is a point of view."

Mace Windu - "He's too dangerous to be left alive."

Anakin - "It's not the Jedi way."

Obi-Wan - "Only a Sith deals in absolutes."

Anakin - "If you're not with me, you're my enemy."

Does any of this rhetoric sound familiar? Have the American people, the world for that matter, ever heard language like this before? Did Michael Moore stumble onto the set in a Jabba the Hut costume?

This theme was as surprising as any am*bush* in the film. Lucas has characters cite "peace, justice, freedom and security" as the rationale for war. That makes pretty good sense... until you see what characters Lucas chooses to deliver the lines. Personally, I found the added political allegory somewhat refreshing, since it implies that Mr. Lucas is not in it *just* for the money.

At 161 minutes, with a PG-13 rating (plenty of violence, loud explosions and an execution), *Revenge of the Sith* is better than the last two *Star Wars* films, but, perhaps not quite as good as the original three and less kid-friendly. On the whole, I really liked the film and loved the Saga. "Miss you, I will, *Star Wars*."

After 28 years of this adventure, now that it is finally over, the last word should not be given by me, or Anakin, or even George. For the last word on *Star Wars* and how to cope with its loss... 'turn to Master Yoda, we must'. In *Revenge of the Sith*, the green sage advises Anakin, "Train yourself to let go of everything you fear to lose." I hope I handle the advice better than Anakin did.

Four light sabers out of five...
****

117

Star Wars: Episode III
Revenge of the Sith
(2005)

Col. 1, first graph:

This is a longer lead than I'd usually write, but let's face it, *SW III*, for many reasons, is a special situation.

Col 1, paragraph 2:

First line: Because this film is surrounded by five other films, I wanted to get the basic plot summary done before I went anywhere else. The 'living on an asteroid in the Naboo Quadrant' line is a touch of local color.

Line 10: Even though everyone pretty much knows what happens to Anakin before entering the theater, I'm still uncomfortable giving it away. So, rather than *say* it, I *ask* it.

Col. 1, paragraph 3:

Line 11: Sometimes it's better to say something less directly, adding a pinch of panache. Here I'm crediting the spectacle, but suggesting that for it to really work its magic, one might have to momentarily mute critical thought.

Line 14: Statement and support. I claim that the "swashbuckling scenario continues throughout the film" and try to quantify it by citing the number of battles. I really did count at least 15 (I made a slash on the upper, right hand corner of my notes every time one began).

Col. 1, last paragraph:

Line 4: While it's important to use quotes from the film, a useful exception would be to create a line of your own, perhaps delivered by one of the characters. "Twisted by the *Green* side, Master Lucas has become."

Col. 2, first graph:

Line 1: In the first draft I had not written, "...Obi driving an Audi." But in working the copy, I played with different characters and different products. This one had a nice ring to it.

Last line: Playing with words, creating a new one to express a concept that's central to the movie... "filmercial". Considering how many people have used so many words for so long, it can be rewarding to think that you've just written something for the first time (even if no one else ever writes it again).

Col. 2, paragraph 2:

Lines 5 & 13: "fitting forbearer" and "deliciously dark" brief touches of alliteration can help move the copy along.

Col. 3, paragraph 2:

Line 4: It's okay to have fun, just do it quickly and not too often.

Col. 3, paragraph 4:

Again, the odds are pretty good that many of your readers are film buffs. If you see something in one film that brings to mind another film, mention it.

Col. 4, paragraph 2 and beyond:

I heard all of these lines spoken in the film. If one considers the events of the day in conjunction with the themes of the film, the lines take on added meaning. And, yes, I really did scribble them onto my pad as I watched the movie.

Col. 4, next to last paragraph:

Since PG-13 ratings are more or less 'tweeners', I usually add a few words as to why they received that rating. As a parent of an 11 and a 13 year old, I appreciate the added info when other critics do it.

Col. 4, last paragraph:

For me, the *only* way to end this review, and by extension the entire series, is to return to the film and let Yoda do it.

Bad Santa

MAKES THIS CRITIC A BELIEVER IN SANTACIDE

by *John Morano*

Bad Santa is bad… really. And not in the sense, "I'm so bad, I'm good." Director Terry Zwigoff's film is vile, crude, sophomoric, and has enough problems to fill Santa's sleigh.

Billy Bob Thronton plays Willie, a department store Santa unlike any you've ever seen before. He makes the Grinch and Scrooge look like sugar plumb fairies. He's the anti-Santa. Willie can't complete a sentence without using the 'f' word, twice. He comes to work drunk and wets himself so much it looks like the North Pole has melted in his lap. His partner in crime, literally, is a felonious elf, played nicely by Tony Cox. The pair have a racquet where they appear annually at a major department store as Santa and his helper, and then, the night before Christmas clean out the store's safe so they can take the rest of the year off.

Even though the film is a nightmare, it does occasionally achieve. Thornton, I hate to admit it, does a solid job as Willie. It's almost like Nicholas Cage in *Leaving Las Vegas* slipped on a Santa suit. Thornton relishes the opportunity to diss virtually everything ole Saint Nick stands for. His portrayal is unbridled, to say the least. In a bar (Where else would you find Santa after hours?) Willie tells an attractive bartender (Lauren Graham), in one of the few lines I can actually print, "I'm an accountant. I wear this thing (Santa suit) as a fashion statement." Later, with a wink and a nod. Willie introduces the bartender as, "Mrs. Santa's sister."

The late John Ritter adds an engaging portrayal of the always politically correct store manager, Bob Chipeska, in what is sadly the actor's final film role. The movie is dedicated to Ritter, although I'm not at all sure it will serve as a fitting legacy.

One other (perhaps the only other) achievement *Bad Santa* manages is that it takes us someplace holiday films have never taken us before. While *Grinch*, *Scrooge* and others of the type have tasted the eggnog of the darker side of the holiday, *Bad Santa* chugs it down with a whiskey chaser. The film is so over-the-top, so outrageous that it's somewhat brave in its attempt. Although that is noteworthy, it's also the film's undoing.

While one *might* find it amusing that Santa neglects to wear his *Depends* once, after three accidents, it gets a little old. And while it *might* be funny to hear Santa utter an expletive here and there, and put a rude child in his/her place, after 20 minutes of incessant cursing and rampant child abuse, the joke's over. *Bad Santa*, however, manages to take us where we've never been, but the film never moves on. It's the same humor, the same jokes for 93 minutes. In the end, it's little more than *South Park* meets Santa.

The camera is instantly forgettable. Other than a shot of Gin, played by Bernie Mac (who doesn't get enough screen time), inhaling a cigarette in one long suck; and a shot of Santa collapsing, as far as the camera is concerned, we might as well be watching a lame TV movie.

The editing and the story are both inconsistent. Cuts from one scene to another are occasionally disjointed and clumsy. The story, written by Glenn Ficarra and John Requa with the Coen brothers, leaves plot lines and characters dangling like empty stockings over the fireplace. In one useless scene, Ajay Naidu plays a homophobic Hindustani who attacks Willie in a parking lot. We never see or hear from him again, nor was he referred to before the scene.

One of the things that bothers me most about the 'R' rated holiday flick, is just that… the rating. I've reviewed, and loved, countless 'R' rated films. I gushed over *Austin Powers*, *Animal House*, *Caddyshack*, *Wayne's World* and too many others to name. But here's what bothers me about the 'R' rated *Bad Santa*, it's Brett Kelly, who plays The Kid. His acting is right on. He does a very nice job. However, what bothers me is that this kid couldn't *see* the film without a parent or guardian. Yet, he can *appear* in it. He stands there, a child, not an adult playing a child, and is subjected to all this garbage in person that he's not allowed to witness without a parent. That's wacky. I know he auditioned, got paid and probably drooled for the

role. I know his parents were probably thrilled for the opportunity. But I'm a dad, and I just don't get, for any amount of money, putting a child into *Bad Santa*.

Is the film totally bad? No. Does it have moments? Absolutely. Is there an audience for it? It's killing in the box office. But in the end, for me, and I'm betting a few other people, I expect more from a film. I don't go to the movies to see road kill. *Bad Santa* takes the easy, obvious way out. If I didn't have to review it, I would have also taken the easy, obvious way out… of the theater.

Bad Santa
(2003)

Col. 1, paragraph 1:

I thought I'd get right to the point here and let readers know exactly where I'm coming from.

Col. 1, paragraph 2:

Grinch, Scrooge, anti-Santa... I'm trying to use some local color, some film/literary images early on.

Lines 10-13: local color.

Col. 1, paragraph 3:

Lines 5-7: I'm looking for a cinematic equivalent to Thornton's role.

Col. 2, paragraph 2:

Lines 11-13: Attempting to be balanced, fair & honest. While I don't like the film, I can still find merit in it.

Col. 2, paragraph 3:

Last two lines: using an image film-goers will likely understand.

Col. 2, last graph:

Lines 7-10: constructing comments built around images that pertain to the film (local color).

Col. 3, top two lines:

'homophobic Hindustani' (alliteration and probably a pretty unique phrase).

Col. 3, first full graph:

Lines 4-9: Trying to establish that I'm not against racy comedies in general. I actually LOVE them (just not this one).

Lines 14-end: Trying to present a thought that many might not consider.

Col. 4, last graph:

Trying to close by being fair, but also making it clear what my standards are and exactly how I feel about the film.

'KONGRATULATIONS' ARE IN ORDER

Epic film delivers

by John Morano

Screenwriter Jack Driscoll (Adrien Brody) looks lovingly at leading lady Ann Darrow (Naomi Watts) and asks in regard to his passion, "Isn't it obvious?" She replies, "I guess I must have missed it." Well, that might be the only thing in Peter Jackson's *King Kong* that isn't obvious. The plot, the effects, the budget, the ambition are all about as obvious as, let's say... a 25ft. gorilla. But in this instance it's actually a strength, not a weakness.

Based on the 1933 original, Jackson deserves 'Kongratulations' for a job well done. This is a Hollywood special effects spectacle of the highest order, just as the original was back in its day.

Not your run of the jungle; ape meets girl, ape gets girl, ape loses girl story, *Kong* is different because of the sheer immensity of the film. Almost everything about it is enormous. If you are planning to see it, this one's a must-see on the big screen. Let's face it, a 15 inch Kong with tinny speakers in your living room just won't cut it.

For those of you who don't already know the story, the movie follows director Carl Denham (Jack Black) on a foray to the infamous Skull Island, where he hopes to shoot on location. While there, the film crew encounters *Jurassic Park*-like dinosaurs, blood thirsty natives and yes, Kong. Long story short (get comfy, this one's 187 minutes), the humans grab the gorilla and Kong winds up on Broadway. Along the way, the big lug falls for Ann Darrow, Denham's star.

As far as the human players go, this is a nice role for Jack Black, who really embraces the part. Looking like a young Orson Welles,

he's a natural to play Denham, a character who's 2/3 filmmaker and 1/3 con man (if one can separate the two). Naomi Watts turns in a fine performance as Ann Darrow. She's perfect for the part and has wonderful chemistry with Kong, really. Perhaps this role will compliment her career as it did for Jessica Lange who played the part in the 1976 Dino De Laurentiis production. Adrien Brody, whose work I generally admire, is serviceable as screenwriter Jack Driscoll, but is somewhat upstaged by both Kong and the sheer spectacle of the film.

Let's face it, the real star here is the ape. It should be pointed out that Andy Serkis, who also plays Lumpy, performed as Kong. He has experience playing computer generated parts as he appeared as Golem in Jackson's *Lord of the Rings* trilogy. Serkis reportedly spent three weeks in the mountains of Rwanda studying gorillas to prepare for the role. And it might just be that blend, that merging of ape and man that makes Kong so touching, so sympathetic a character. It's one of Jackson's biggest successes, the hint of humanization in Kong that suggests how much we have in common with this creature.

But as Kong becomes more exposed to humans, the great silverback softens the edge that has kept him alive in the wild. Ironically, while the ape becomes more human, the humans generally become more like animals in their treatment of Kong. Ann becomes an unwitting femme fatale. She does feel deeply for Kong, but I was waiting for her to deliver the classic line to the pouty primate, "I just don't feel that way about you. You're more like a brother to me. Can we be friends?"

While Darrow's no Diane Fossey, one would hope that some viewers, if they did feel something for Kong, would take things a step further and consider the plight of his cousins the Mountain Gorilla and the Lowland Gorilla of south-central Africa. There are no shortage of environmental groups dedicated to helping these magnificent, albeit extremely endangered, creatures; World Wildlife Fund, The Gorilla Foundation and African Wildlife Foundation among them.

There are many memorable scenes in the film; Kong rumbling with raptors and later pursuing a fleeing Ann, the depictions of 1930's New York and Denham greeting guests triumphantly on Broadway are a few. One of my favorite scenes, however, is not the most spectacular. It takes place when Kong and Ann sit outside his mountain cave and share a sunset, watching it descend on the jungle below. It's simple, quiet, peaceful and stunning. The vision stands in satisfying contrast to the rest of the film. Moments later, as Driscoll attempts to rescue Ann, the peace is shattered and so is Kong's world.

When we return to New York, we see the real jungle. Both Manhattan Island and Skull Island are awesome spectacles through Jackson's lens, and at times are equally perilous.

In reading the production notes for *King Kong*, after the four pages of cast and crew

credits you come to the special effects people. This is the first time in my experience that I've seen SEVEN PAGES of people listed just for effects, illustrating what the film is built upon.

Rated PG-13, the film does have some dicey moments that don't warrant and R, but might make younger movie goes a little restless when they try to go to sleep that night. Most of them take place, predictably, on Skull Island.

In the final minutes, when Kong climbs the Empire State Building and battles a squadron of bi-planes, things get a little confusing. Jackson loses count of how many planes he began with (5), how many are lost and how many remain. Driscoll walking through a police line outside the building and casually taking an elevator to the top floor also makes the scene less believable. But the incredible shots of Manhattan below and Kong battling the aerial onslaught tend to diminish the lapses in continuity, a concept that generally holds true throughout the film. For example, giant insects on Skull Island are machine-gunned while they attempt to ingest unlucky crew members. Miraculously, only the insects are shot.

Toward the close, with Kong perched atop the Empire State Building, Ann calling to him from the observation deck, I half expected the ape to rise up and speak, saying in a *Brokeback Mountain-Gorilla* homage, "Ann Darrow, I can't quit you!" Of course, that doesn't happen, and most of us know what does.

On Broadway, Carl Denham introduces his Kong as, "THE EIGHTH WONDER OF THE WORLD!" Although Peter Jackson's film doesn't quite reach that plateau, it does make one wonder, with the current state of computer graphics and filmmaking, what can't be done on screen? Ironically, it's the same question, sans the computer, that movie-goes asked in 1933 when they saw the original film. This latest version is a fitting follow-up to what the original began where B-movie monsters are given A-list treatment.

4 out of 5 stars

What films are making a play to win some Oscars...

BROKEBACK MOUNTAIN
A love affair between two male cowboys

CRASH
Racially charged drama

WALK THE LINE
Johnny Cash meets June Carter on screen

GOOD NIGHT AND GOOD LUCK
The story of "McCarthyism"

CONSTANT GARDENER
A tale of drug company chicanery in Africa

SYRIANA
A Middle Eastern oil plot

MUNICH
Israel and Palestinean conflict

CAPOTE
The story of the famous "new journalist"

KING KONG
The big guy, uh, ape

King Kong

(2006)

Col. 1, paragraph 1:

Using a situation and two quotes to construct the lead.

Col. 1, paragraph 2:

'Kongratulations'... you'll never find it in the dictionary, but I love to play with words and I think it applies.

Col. 1, paragraph 3:

Lines 5 & 6: While it's not true for most films, this one requires the big screen to get the full effect.

Col. 1, paragraph 4:

It's not too hard to give a plot synopsis quickie in one paragraph.

Line 6: J-Park dinos... I'm using an image from another film.

Line 8: I like to use parenthetical asides. Just don't overuse them.

Col. 2, top graph:

Lines 6-9: *Kong* has history, so don't ignore it. I mentioned it in the lead and close as well.

Col. 2, second full graph:

Line 10: a touch of alliteration.

Don't Tell Me the Ending!

Col. 2, third full graph:

Don't be afraid to interpret the film and point out civic conclusions that might be lost on filmmakers and/or viewers.

Col. 3, first full graph:

Consider younger viewers and parents. This rating needs a little extra discussion.

Col. 3, second full graph:

Last six lines: Have a little fun. Work in another contemporary blockbuster.

Col. 3, last graph:

Sum it up with some style... spectacle, history, effects... check, please. That's it.

Passionate About Christ
A BRUTAL JOURNEY OF FORGIVENESS AND HOPE

by John Morano

When I was first asked to review Mel Gibson's *The Passion of the Christ*, I backed off the assignment. I explained that I was not a biblical scholar and would not be able to discuss how accurate Gibson's portrayal was... Then I saw the film. The next day I made a phone call accepting the assignment.

First things first... Does Mel Gibson have a right to make *The Passion*? Does he have a right to invest $25 million of his own money to produce the film? If Martin Scorsese can make *The Last Temptation of Christ* (1988), if Norman Jewison can make *Jesus Christ Superstar* (1973), if Nicholas Ray can make *King of Kings* (1961); well, then it would seem that Mel Gibson has a right to shoot his film.

It's important to keep in mind that just as any production of Shakespeare's *King Lear* is an interpretation, so too is Gibson's vision of the crucifixion. And that's what this film is, the story of Christ's crucifixion. Gibson looks at little that happened before the arrest and even less that occurred after the entombment. The resurrection is a virtual afterthought in this film.

The Passion is really about the suffering that Christ endured. The 'R' rating is for violence (not 'R'eligion) that is graphic and in your face. As someone who found the '39 Lashes' sequence in *Jesus Christ Superstar* disturbing; seeing Christ chained to a whipping post and flogged mercilessly for what seemed like 3339 lashes, I couldn't help but look away during some of the more savage sequences.

But to be honest, the brutality is vital to Gibson's portrayal and it helped me understand that Jesus suffered unimaginable torture long *before* he was nailed to the cross. That alone gives the film value. It is the depiction of the ferocious barbarity inflicted on Christ that separates The Passion from other films that examine the crucifixion. Gibson takes us to a place we've never been before.

From what I've read and heard Gibson's version of the crucifixion is, for the most part, accurate. It's certainly more accurate than Oliver Stone's *JFK* (1991) or *Nixon* (1995). The director has made several decisions that seem to illustrate his desire for authenticity. He told his story in Aramaic, Latin and Hebrew with subtitles, foregoing the cliche' British accented performances we've all seen before. He filmed mostly on location in Italy, giving the film a faithful feel. Caleb Deschanel's camera is creative, clean and convincing. John Wright's editing moves the 127 minute feature along at a satisfying pace. Carlo Gervasi's set design and Maurizio Millenotti's costume design increase the actor's's credibility. In short, Gibson's $25 million film looks more like $75 million.

Pursuing the idea of accuracy, many have complained that *The Passion* is an indictment of Jews. If that's true, then it's also an indictment of Romans. But I didn't see it that way. For me, the film is not about blame. If you walk out of the theater seeing that Gibson has blamed

The Passion of the Christ
(Newmarket Film Group)
Starring: James Caviezel, Monica Bellucci, Rosalinda Celentano
"R"
For sequences of graphic violence
★★★★★

the Jews for Christ's demise, I would argue two things. One, you probably walked into the film thinking that. Two, you never actually saw the film. This movie's about faith, suffering, sacrifice, forgiveness and so much more. To me, *The Passion* says that this was God's plan. The Jews, the Romans, the Disciple who denied their association to Jesus were all doing God's will. You can't blame them for that.

Gibson also makes it clear that the devil had a hand in the crucifixion as well. Satan, played with unsettling understatement by Rosalinda Celentano, lurked in the crowd, in the courts and at the cross. James Caviezel was outstanding as Jesus, especially considering some of the demands the director placed on him to perform the part.

One of the things that struck me most deeply about *The Passion* happened just before the film began and the moment it was over. I attended a late night screening and chose a seat all alone in the center of the theater. Another man walked in moments before the film began. He strolled up the stairs, stopped at my aisle walked towards me, smiled and sat one seat over from me. I couldn't believe that in an

^ ***The Passion* tells the story of the last 12 hours of Jesus' life.**

empty theater, this guy would invade my space. I tried to ignore him, but during the film he'd occasionally lean over and say things like, "wow... cool... what a scene." I really didn't want to chat with anyone, especially a stranger, while the film was running.

When it was over, I gathered my things. The young man extended his hand and said, "What a film." I shook his hand and agreed. Then he asked me, "Are you born again?" He said it in a very nice, unthreatening way, not at all the 'I have a pamphlet that will change your life' delivery. I told him that I was a Christian. We spoke about faith and film for a few moments on our walk to the parking lot. And then we went our own separate ways.

In my life I've covered more films than I can count. I've worked the entertainment beats in New York and Los Angeles and other places not so big. And, in 25 years of covering films, I never walked out of the theater discussing my faith and Christ with a stranger. That's what *The Passion of the Christ* is about. That's what Mel Gibson has achieved. ✪

ndmag.com April 2004 Page 81

The Passion of the Christ
(2004)

Col. 1, paragraph 1:

This is a personal, anecdotal lead. Later in the review, I'll return to what I started here.

Col. 1, paragraph 2:

Nodding to the inverted pyramid and addressing one of the main points of contention about the film, it seemed important to get this out of the way up front.

Col. 1, paragraph 4:

Lines 3 & 4: This is about as much fun as I can have with a film like *The Passion*.

Lines 6-8: Again, trying to consider similar productions.

Last line: a quick sprinkle of alliteration.

Col. 2, first full graph:

Lines 6-11: Looking for films/directors that might not come from the religious perspective, but that have taken license with historical perspectives.

Col. 2, last graph:

Try not to duck uncomfortable debate. I usually like to meet it head-on. It makes for interesting reading and tests one's mettle as a critic.

Col. 3, last graph:

I'm actually starting my close here. This is not at all the norm for me, but again, your style should be flexible. In this situation it made sense. This close, like the lead, is anecdotal in construction.

Col. 4, last graph:

This is the full-blown close. I've used a mutant two-step close, moving from two anecdotal graphs to one final summary graph. It worked for me.

CAPOTE

Oscar worthy film

by John Morano

The first time I'd ever been asked to see Capote, I was in college in 1980 and my basketball coach *requested* that the team attend a reading by the author. I wasn't very eager to listen to a writer whom I had never heard of, especially since the event was scheduled for a Friday night. When Truman sashayed onto the stage wearing long purple robes and a matching safari hat, appearing less than sober, I was convinced the evening would be an incredible waste of time.

I sat in the front row with the rest of the team. Capote's strange whiney voice, annoying at first, eventually carried me away. I was absorbed by the narration. When he finished reading *A Christmas Memory*, I was in tears, literally, and I couldn't really explain why. I rose and walked down the center aisle of the theater, the nation's leading rebounder comforting me as I cried. The rest of the university watched their weeping shooting guard and wondered whether the Cougars would win a game that year.

While the Cougars did win a game (30 of them actually), I learned something very important that night. I wanted to be a writer. Seeing what Capote could do with nothing but words on a page changed my life. So, when I was asked some 25 years later to see *Capote*, I didn't hesitate. And while the film did not change my life, as the author did, the evening in the theater was very well spent.

Director Bennett Miller's film (apparently his feature debut) generally concerns itself with the events leading up to and surrounding how Truman Capote created his groundbreaking non-fiction novel, *In Cold Blood*. For those who aren't familiar with *In Cold Blood*, it's a story about the slaying of the Clutter's, a farming family from Holcomb, Kansas who were murdered in their home by Perry Smith and Dick Hickock in 1959.

Early in the film we see Capote (Philip Seymour Hoffman) scanning the NY Times, reading an article about the crime,

picking up a pair of scissors and clipping it from the paper. This is one of the most rewarding elements of the film, the illusion that you're a fly on the wall watching Capote work, getting an inside look into his fascinating life.

Later, he tells friend and fellow author Harper Lee (Catherine Keener) that he wants his book, "... to return Perry to the realm of humanity." In a sense, the film attempts to do the same for Capote. When all is said and done, the viewer has a better understanding of why the writer lived the way he did. Perhaps one of the reasons he relied on alcohol and drugs to the destructive degree that he did, stems from the deep guilt he felt over the way he used Perry and Dick to write his book. And so, when Capote wrote in *In Cold Blood*, "...four shotgun blasts... ended six human lives," one could argue that the number should actually be seven, because in some measure Capote's life was lost as well.

Truman says, "Ever since I was a child, folks have thought they had me pegged, because of the way I am, the way I talk. And they're always wrong." They might've been wrong, but the film is generally dead on. The two people most directly responsible for the air of authenticity are Bennett Miller and Philip Seymour Hoffman's haunting incarnation of Truman. These are Oscar worthy efforts from both. It's also important to note the solid literary foundation, vital in a film like this, provided by Gerald Cook's book and Dan Futterman's screenplay.

Capote is an unabashed success on so many levels, not just artistically, but also as a film about writing and journalism. However, Capote's method, at best, is really pseudo journalism. When he comments about Perry, saying, "He's a gold mine." We're reminded that the writer is not performing a public service. He expects this book to line his pockets and energize his career. Drawn to promotion like a moth to a flame, ready to mix a martini in the morning at the drop of an ice cube, we see the writer lie to sources and manipulate others in order to extract the information he so desperately desires. Ultimately, we're forced to wonder just who the real criminal in the cell is, Perry or Truman?

When Capote's publisher, William Shawn (Bob Balaban), boasts that his client's book is, "... going to change the way people write," he's somewhat on target. Surely, writers like Norman Mailer, Joseph Wambaugh, Tom Wolfe, Joan Didion, Joe McGinniss and others were all influenced by *In Cold Blood*.

But the film is about so much more than writing. It's a story of pain, death, ambition, grief, friendship and more. *Capote* is a tour-de-force for Hoffman, a signature performance. It's difficult to imagine another actor doing a more brilliant job. Hoffman's transformation is complete and compelling. In addition, Catherine Keener's Harper Lee is wonderful and deep. The chemistry between Keener and Hoffman is genuine (Capote actually dedicated *In Cold Blood* to Lee and Jack Dunphy). It's also important to recognize Clifton

Collins Jr. as Perry Smith. Taking nothing away from Robert Blake and Eric Stoltz's incarnations (1967 & 1996, respectively), Collins' portrayal is sophisticated and gripping.

The production values are all there. Whether filming in New York, Kansas or Spain, the sets and characters consistently ring true. Cinematographer Adam Kimmel provides plenty of close-ups that pull you into the frame, punctuating intimate moments. You lean over the prison table with Truman and hear him whisper a question to Perry. There's a wonderful arrest/booking scene, a montage deftly edited by Christopher Tellefsen, that keeps the film rolling along, but also tends to skip over the initial trial. I wondered whether the coffin scene at the Clutter's wake was necessary (and factual). And the final scenes will bring to mind the 1967 cinematic, *In Cold Blood*.

At 130 minutes, *Capote* does not drag. It is rightly rated R for language, some graphic violence and adult themes. The film will likely play better to people who are familiar with Capote and his work, especially if you've ever turned the pages or creased the binding of *In Cold Blood*.

Asked about the success of Harper Lee's newly released novel at a swank New York cocktail party, Truman replies, "I don't frankly see what all the fuss is about." Well, having seen the film *Capote*, I understand what all the fuss is about. Bennett Miller and Philip Seymour Hoffman have created a film that's magic and memorable.

Capote

(2005)

Col. 1, first three graphs:

    This is a very long anecdotal lead, not typical for me at all, But this is a unique situation. I had a genuine Capote moment, one that might affect my feelings for the film. With both those things in mind, I felt I had to seize the moment and run with it.

Col. 1, paragraphs 4, 5, 6, etc.

    In this review, I've extended the amount of plot synopsis that I usually use. This is more or less a true story that has been discussed for forty years. It's also something I've taught, so I chose to prolong plot, without hopefully giving too much away or boring the reader.

Col. 1, last paragraph:

    Since the film attempts to give us an inside look into Capote's life, I tried to do the same in that graph.

Col. 2, first full graph:

    Lines 13-15: Knowing the book can add depth to your review. In a film like this, reading *In Cold Blood* is a must.

Col. 2, last graph:

    Lines 1-4: Listen to the film. See if you can hear a quote that states a theme, then use it.

Col. 3, top graph:

Lines 12 & 13: Make images your own. While the preceding line is somewhat cliché, the following line is totally original and appropriate to the content of the film. Try to leave *your* thumbprint, not someone else's on *your* words.

Lines 13-16: Here I'm trying to be vaguely specific.

Col. 3, last 3 lines onto top of Col. 4:

Again, know the text. I would never have known about the dedication had I not checked Capote's book. Also, don't forget to credit outstanding supporting players and to keep the film's cinematic history on your radar.

Col. 4, first full graph:

Lines 4 & 5 and 11 & 12: When production elements strike you, remember that there are people responsible for what you've seen/heard. Credit them by name.

Lines 13 to end: As much as I liked the film, it was not perfect. Always try to point out the cracks in the armor. In the end it'll give you more credibility and you won't look like a fan that has lost the ability to be critical.

Col. 4, last graph:

I toyed with the idea of returning to the lead, but decided not to. There's already more of me than I'd usually like in a review. Instead, I went with a 'nuts & bolts' closing that uses a quote from the movie to leave no doubt where I stand on the film. Often, less is more.

Notes

Introduction:

1) Truffaut, Francois, *The Films of My Life*, (Simon and Schuster, 1978) pg. 12
2) Dornenburg, Andrew & Page, Karen, *Dining Out*, (John Wiley & Sons, 1998), pg 162
3) Amberg, George, *New York Times Film Reviews 1913-1970* (Arno Press, 1971)
4) Simon, John, *Singularities: Essays on the Theater 1964-1974* (Random House, 1975) pg. 223 & 225
5) Bywater, Tim & Sobchack, Thomas, *Introduction to Film Criticism* (Longman, 1989) pg. 5 & pg. 22
6) Kauffman, Stanley, "Why I'm Not Bored," *The New Republic* (1974)
7) Truffaut, Francois, *The Films in My Life*, (Simon and Schuster, 1978) pg. 3
8) Kael, Pauline, *For Keeps:30 Years at the Movies* (Penguin, 1994), pg. Intro
9) Ebert, Roger, *Roger Ebert's Book of Film* (Norton, 1997) pg. 13

Chapter 1:

1) Simon, John, *Singularities: Essays on the Theater 1964-1974* (Random House, 1975) pg. 97
2) Shakespeare, William, *Hamlet*, Act I, Scene III, Lines 78-80
3) Seligman, Craig, *Sontag & Kael: Opposites Attract Me*, (Counterpoint, 2004) pg. 188
4) Simon, John, *Singularities: Essays on the Theater 1964-1974* (Random House, 1975) pg. 226
5) Dornenburg, Andrew & Page, Karen, *Dining Out*, (John Wiley & Sons, 1998) pg. 176
6) Seligman, Craig, *Sontag & Kael: Opposites Attract Me*, (Counterpoint, 2004) pg. 172
7) Maslin, Janet, "Inside the *New York Times*," (Fall, 1998, Vol. 2. No. 3, Promo Dept. NYT)
8) Seligman, Craig, *Sontag & Kael: Opposites Attract Me*, (Counterpoint, 2004) pg. 7
9) Safer, Morely, *CBS News: 60 Minutes "The Critic,"* (CBS, 3/17/91)
10) Truffaut, Francois, *The Films of My Life*, (Simon and Schuster, 1978) pg. 12
11) Murrow, Edward R., *American Masters: This Reporter* (PBS, 8/06)
12) Truffaut, Francois, *Hitchcock*, (Simon and Schuster, 1967) pg. 115
13) Lane, Anthony, "Bombs Away," (*The New Yorker*, 6/4/01) pg. 82
14) Kael, Pauline, *For Keeps:30 Years at the Movies* (Penguin, 1994) pg. 1107
15) Simon, John, *Singularities: Essays on the Theater 1964-1974* (Random House, 1975) pg. 211

16) Truffaut, Francois,

17) Parales, John, *Special to the Times II*, (*New York Times* Video, 11/92)

18) Douglas, Susan, *Behind the Screens: Hollywood Goes Hypercommercial* (Media Education Foundation, 2002)

19) McChesney, Robert W., *Behind the Screens: Hollywood Goes Hypercommercial* (Media Education Foundation, 2002)

20) Ebert, Roger, *Roger Ebert's Book of Film*, (Norton, 1997) pg. 14

21) Amberg, George, *The New York Times Film Reviews 1913-1970*, (Arno, 1971), pg. Viii

22) Buckland, Warren, *Teach Yourself: Film Studies*, (Contemporary Books, 2003), pg. 88

23) Buckland, Warren, *Teach Yourself: Film Studies*, (Contemporary Books, 2003), pg. 20

Chapter 2:

1) Truffaut, Francois, "We Must Continue Making Progress," *Film: A Montage of Theories*. Ed. Richard Dyer MacCann, (Dutton, 1966), pg. 370

2) Simon, John, *Singularities: Essays on the Theater 1964-1974*, (Random House, 1975) pg. 81

3) Morano, John, "*Biloxi Blues* Captures Simon's Youth," (*Center Daily Times*, 1986)

4) Morano, John, "Gance's *Napoleon* Conquers Screen," (*the Scarlet,* et1980)

5) Morano, John, "Star Trek," (*Inside Books*, December 1988) pg. 50

6) Kael, Pauline, *For Keeps: 30 Years at the Movies*, (Penguin, 1994) pg. 877 & 878

7) Bordwell, David, *The McGraw-Hill Film Viewer's Guide*, (McGraw-Hill, 2001) pg. 15

8) Kael, Pauline, *For Keeps: 30 Years at the Movies*, (Penguin, 1994) pg. 764 & 766

9) Morano, John, "Gance's *Napoleon* Conquers Screen," (*the Scarlet,* 1980)

10) Kael, Pauline, *For Keeps: 30 Years at the Movies*, (Penguin, 1994) pg. 765

11) Kael, Pauline, *For Keeps: 30 Years at the Movies*, (Penguin, 1994) pg. 1224

Chapter 3:

1) Kael, Pauline, *I Lost It at the Movies*, (Bantam Books, 1965) pgs. 277-278

2) Kael, Pauline, *For Keeps: 30 Years at the Movies*, (Penguin, 1994) pg. 1223

3) Kauffmann, Stanley, "Why I'm Not Bored," *The New Republic* (1974)

4) Thompson, Anne, "Criticism's Status Quo Getting Thumbs Down," *The Hollywood Reporter* .com (June 2, 2006)

5) Thompson, Anne, "Criticism's Status Quo Getting Thumbs Down," *The Hollywood*

Reporter .com (June 2, 2006)

6) O'Sullivan, Eleanor, "Critics are Feeling the Studio Squeeze," (*Asbury Park Press,* 8/27/06) E-1

7) Kael, Pauline, *For Keeps: 30 Years at the Movies,* (Penguin, 1994) pg. Intro.

8) Biagi, Shirley, *Newstalk I,* (Wadsworth, 1987) pg. 198

9) Bordwell, David, *The McGraw-Hill Film Viewer's Guide,* (McGraw-Hill, 2001) pg. 11

10) Morano, John, "Mr. & Mrs. Smith Sizzles... and Fizzles," (*Night & Day Magazine,* 2005) pg. 53

11) Bordwell, David, *The McGraw-Hill Film Viewer's Guide,* (McGraw-Hill, 2001) pg. 5

12) Morano, John, "*Biloxi Blues* Captures Simon's Youth," (*Center Daily Times,* 1986)

13) Morano, John, "No Need to Dodge *Dodgeball*," (*Night & Day Magazine,* 2004) pg. 68

14) Marx, Bill, "The Floundering State of Film Criticism," (WBUR, Boston: wbur.org 11/22/05

15) Corrigan, Timothy, *A Short Guide to Writing About Film,* (Pearson Longman, 2004) pg. 3

Chapter 4:

1) Simon, John, *Singularities: Essays on the Theater 1964-1974,* (Random House, 1975) pg. 95

2) Morano, John, "Thespians' *Cabaret* a Bit Uneven," (*Center Daily Times,* 3/28/87) pg. B-8

3) Simon, John, *Singularities: Essays on the Theater 1964-1974* (Random House, 1975) pg. 82

Chapter 5:

1) Harmetz, Aljean, "Film Junkets for Journalists Raising Divisive Questions," *The New York Times,* (3/19/78) pg. 54

2) Goodwin, H. Eugene, *Groping for Ethics in Journalism,* (Iowa State Univ. Press, 1983) pg. 100

3) Phillips, Richard, "The Culture of Independent Film Criticism Has Gone Down the Drain," (World Socialist Web Site: wsws.org 1/10/00)

4) *Sigma Delta Chi, The Society of Professional Journalists,* Code of Ethics, (adopted 1926, revised 1984)

5) Biagi, Shirley, *Newstalk I,* (Wadsworth, 1987) pg. 200

6) Faraci, Devon, "Exclusive Interview: Phillip Lopate," (CHUD.com, 5/10/06)

7) Biagi, Shirley, *Newstalk I,* (Wadsworth, 1987) pg. 199

8) *Film Critics Draw Fire for Accepting Studio Money,* Associated Press, March 8, 1992

9) *Film Critics Draw Fire for Accepting Studio Money,* Associated Press, March 8, 1992

10) Miller, Mark Crispin, *Behind the Screens: Hollywood Goes Hypercommercial,* (The Media Education Foundation, 2002)

11) Wolper, Allan, "Two Thumbs Down on Blurbing, U.S.A." *Editor & Publisher,* (January, 2004) pg. 21

12) Wolper, Allan, "Two Thumbs Down on Blurbing, U.S.A." *Editor & Publisher,* (January, 2004) pg. 21

13) Porter & Ferris, *The Practice of Journalism,* (Prentice Hall, 1988) pg. 319

14) Seligman, Craig, *Sontag & Kael: Opposites Attract Me,* (Counterpoint, 2004) pg. 187

15) Safer, Morely, *CBS News: 60 Minutes* "The Critic," (CBS 3/17/91)

16) Marx, Bill, "The Floundering State of Film Criticism," (WBUR, Boston: wbur.org 11/22/05)

17) Gleiberman, Owen, "Ask the Critic," *Entertainment Weekly* (June 16, 2006) pg. 55

Chapter 6:

1) Rivers, William L., *Writing Opinion: Reviews,* (Iowa State Univ. Press, 1988) pg. 68

2) Kael, Pauline, *I Lost It at the Movies,* (Bantam Books, 1965) pg. 279

3) Sarris, Andrew, *Confessions of a Cultist: On the Cinema 1955-1969,* (Simon & Schuster, 1970)

4) Biagi, Shirley, *Newstalk I,* (Wadsworth, 1987) pg. 196

5) Maslin, Janet, "Inside the *New York Times,*" (Fall, 1988, Vol. 2, No. 3, Promo Dept. NYT)

6) Faraci, Devon, "Exclusive Interview: Phillip Lopate," (CHUD.com 5/10/06)

7) Maslin, Janet, "Inside the *New York Times,*" (Fall, 1988, Vol. 2, No. 3, Promo Dept. NYT)

About the Author

John Morano is a journalism professor at Monmouth University in New Jersey, where he has taught *Writing the Review* and other journalism courses for almost 20 years. Morano served as Managing Editor of *Modern Screen Magazine* in New York, Editor-in-Chief of *ROCKbeat Magazine* in Los Angeles and Senior Editor of *Inside Books Magazine* in New York/Miami. His freelance pieces have appeared in *Movie Mirror, Editor & Publisher Magazine, The Center Daily Times, Shorelines, Night & Day Magazine* and many other publications.

Prof. Morano is the author of three novels: *A Wing and a Prayer, Makoona* and *Out There, Somewhere*; all part of the *Morano Eco-Adventure Series* published by Blue Works, the young adult imprint of Windstorm Creative.

About Windstorm Creative

Windstorm Creative was founded in 1989 to create a publishing house with author-centric ethics and cutting-edge, risk-taking innovation. Windstorm is now a company of more than ten divisions with international distribution channels that allow us to sell our books both inside the traditional systems and outside these paradigms, capitalizing on more direct delivery and non-traditional markets. As a result, our books can be found in grocery superstores as well as your favorite neighborhood bookstore, and dozens of other outlets on and off the Internet.

Windstorm is an independent press with the synergy and branding of a corporate publisher and an author royalty that's easily twice their best offer. We have continued to minimize returns without decreasing sales by publishing books that are timeless, as opposed to timely, and never back-listing.

Windstorm is constantly changing, improving, and growing. We are driven by the needs of our authors – hailing from ten different countries – and the vision of our critically-acclaimed staff. All of our books are created with the strictest of environmental protections in mind. Our approach to no-waste, no-hazard, in-house production, and stringent out-source scrutiny, assures that our goals are met whether books are printed at our own facility or an outside press.

Visit our webcenter and take 20% off every title, every day. No strings. No fine print. Thank you for supporting an independent press.

Visit
www.WindstormCreative.com
for other excellent nonfiction titles
from fine art to programming
and everything in-between